Additional Advance Praise For
ONE ANOTHERING, VOLUME 2

"Simply the best book for starting a small group that I
know of. Each chapter is a 'stand alone' lesson with personal stories, a biblical principle, and great questions to
use with your own group. *Volume 1* and *Volume 2* can be
used separately or together to learn why and how to
build healthy community."

> —Marjory Zoet Bankson, President,
> Faith At Work; Author, *The Call to the Soul*

"Dick Meyer sets the playing field, outlines the game
rules, and tosses hittable batting practice for small
groups who want to work on their relational game.
With clear, simple, accessible, and practical coaching,
he guides small groups into the depth and complexity
of biblical life together. With a stadium full of great stories, he helps reform rough-hewn gatherings into spar-
kling communal diamonds. Truly a disciple's guide to
good groups."

> —Rev. Dr. Gareth W. Icenogle, Senior Pastor,
> First Presbyterian Church, Bethlehem, PA;
> Adjunct Professor, Fuller Theological Seminary

"This book is about Christian community as it was
meant to be. In his beautiful and often touching stories,
Dick Meyer leads us into a virtual community where
people truly love and care for one another. Dick is a
preacher, but his book doesn't sound preachy. He is de-
lightfully human and mischievously candid."

> —Lyman Coleman, President, Serendipity House

One Anothering, Volume 2

One Anothering
Volume 2

*Building
Spiritual
Community
in Small Groups*

Rev. Richard C. Meyer

Augsburg Books
MINNEAPOLIS

ONE ANOTHERING, VOLUME 2
Building Spiritual Community in Small Groups

First Augsburg Books edition 2006

Large-quantity purchases or custom editions of this book are available at a discount from the publisher. For more information, contact the sales department at Augsburg Fortress, Publishers, 1-800-328-4648, or write to: Sales Director, Augsburg Fortress, Publishers, P. O. Box 1209, Minneapolis, MN 55440-1209.

All biblical references are from the New Revised Standard Version Bible (NRSV) unless otherwise noted. Permission credits are given on page 157.

Cover image: © Royalty-Free/Corbis. Cover design by Diana Running.

ISBN 0-8066-9056-9

The paper used in this publication meets the minimum requirements of American National Standard for Information Sciences—Permanence of Paper for Printed Library Materials, ANSI Z329.48-1984. ♾ ™

Printed in the U. S. A.

08   07   2   3   4   5   6   7   8   9   10

*To the saints at First Presbyterian Church of Maitland
and to my wife, Trudy, the foremost "one anotherer" in my life.*

Contents

Thanks . . .

To Pat Tipton, for her encouragement and her help in contacting publishers for copyright permissions.

To Trudy Meyer, Sarah Chapman, and Gareth Icenogle, whose perceptive comments caused me to rewrite this material more times than I would have on my own.

To Doris Hill, for her patient help with proofreading.

To my editor, Marcia Broucek, for her wise counsel and for the way she improved all the drafts.

To the Faith At Work community of faith, who got me started writing in the first place.

To all the people with whom I have been in a small group, for their giving me so many stories to tell.

INTRODUCTION

According to recent Gallup Institute research, forty percent of all Americans currently meet in a small group for caring and support. I participate in four such groups: a Tuesday night group with my wife, a Friday lunch group with a handful of men, a Tuesday morning group with my office staff, and a monthly clergy support group. The people in these groups have become part of my extended family. We share our lives with one another. We pray for one another. We study together. We encourage one another. We challenge one another. We also disappoint and frustrate one another from time to time. We stick together, however, for two reasons: We want to deepen our relationship with God, and we want to experience community.

The desire for community has been planted deep within us. God created us with a longing for one another. I still remember the time I packed my belongings into my Volkswagen Beetle and moved to Boise, Idaho. I was twenty-two years old, a recent graduate of UCLA, and engaged to be married. I bid farewell to my soon-to-be-wife, Trudy, got into the car, and drove away, looking at her in my rear view mirror. I did well for a while, but somewhere between Los Angeles and Boise, in one of the many the barren stretches of western Nevada, I had an overwhelming need for company. I missed Trudy. I missed Los Angeles. I missed my friends. So I did something I had never done before and have not done since: I picked up a hitchhiker, and we traveled together for two hundred miles until it was time to stop for the night. I do not remember the hitchhiker's name. I only remember how good it was to have someone close by.

The *Los Angeles Times* has a slogan on its masthead: "We're here for you every day." Deep in our hearts we want to know someone is *here for us*. We want to know that we are not alone. We want to know because we were created for community.

I hope this book helps you to experience the joy of community. In 1990 I wrote *One Anothering, Volume 1*, which is a small group starter series. *Volume 1* explored eight of the New Testament "one another" passages with accompanying small group discussion and sharing questions. The "one another" passages in the Bible are addressed to God's people. They are God's blueprint for Christian community. *Volume 1* has proven to be a practical and useful resource for small group leaders and first-time small group participants.

This book continues and expands upon the work of the first volume. The first chapter of *One Anothering, Volume 2*, "The Power of Community," underscores the biblical and theological foundations of Christian community. The following ten chapters contain "one another" studies for a small group.

Prior to your first meeting together, I would recommend that group members read the first two chapters. If you have not previously read *Volume 1*, I suggest you stick closely to the allotted times for group questions at the end of each chapter. Also, remember to begin and end the group on time, and above all, honor confidentiality. Keep what is shared with the group in the group!

In addition, if this is a new group, be sensitive to the time for group prayer at the end of each session. Praying in a group can be intimidating for some. In light of that, I have attempted to "ease" people into group prayer. Even if your group has been meeting for a while and are comfortable praying together, you might want to experiment with the different types of group prayer suggested at the end of the first few chapters. Above all, have fun getting to know each other better.

A number of summers ago, a friend gave me a book, saying, "I thought of you when I read it. Enjoy!" Enjoy I did. *All Summer Long* is the story of three men—a television journalist, a schoolteacher, and a wheeling-and-dealing CEO—who were best friends when they were boys. One summer they decided to put their careers on hold to see if they could rekindle the most cherished times of their youth. Prior to that decision, however, the three of them engaged in a discussion about the old TV show, "The Millionaire." In each episode of the show, John Beresford Tipton, the millionaire, gave away a cashier's check for a million dollars to unsuspecting recipients. Tipton, however, never appeared on screen. Instead, one of his employees always delivered the check.

As the three friends shared their memories of the show, one of them suggested that someone should make a spin-off in which a guy would show up, knock on your door, snap his fingers and, instead of giving you money, would give you permission to take off with your best friends for the summer. One of the guys asked if the new show would be a hit? "Sure," said another. "The payoff's better. The guy on 'The Millionaire' only offered money."[1]

Some things are worth more than money—authentic, vibrant Christian community, for example. I hope this book helps you experience it.

CHAPTER ONE

THE POWER OF COMMUNITY

I was at the Omaha Marriott for a breakfast meeting. I was late and did not want to be distracted, but they sang so enthusiastically. A sign on the door said they were Avon representatives. I peeked into the room they had rented for their meeting. At least five hundred women were on their feet, swaying, clapping, and singing. I picked up a copy of their song. It was printed on pink paper. The sheet read:

AVON SONG
We all belong together
So let's celebrate
Today's another day
When things were simply great.

What a happy feeling
To have come so far
By doing what we love to
What a lucky bunch we are.

We belong
We are Avon
And we're proud . . .
We belong.

Deep within us is a desire to belong. Each of us likes to belong to a group of people where, in the words of the theme song from the sitcom *Cheers*, "everybody knows your name." Some have called it our tribal instinct. Barbra Streisand sold millions of records singing about it. The lyrics "People, who need people, are the luckiest people in the world," struck a responsive chord in the hearts of many. Employees stay on jobs because of it. Even though they might earn more money elsewhere, they stay where they are because they feel like a valued member of a team.

Some have also demonstrated the devastating effects that *not* belonging can have on us. Dean Ornish, M.D., is the President and Director of the Preventative Medicine Research Institute at the University of California's School of Medicine in San Francisco. He has spent a lifetime studying heart disease, and he has demonstrated ways that coronary heart disease can be reversed without the use of drugs or surgery. In an interview with Bill Moyers he said, "I am coming to believe that anything that promotes isolation leads to chronic stress and, in turn, may lead to illnesses like heart disease. Anything that promotes a sense of intimacy, community, and connection, can be healing."[1]

In another Bill Moyers' interview, Rachel Naomi Remen, M.D., made reference to the work of Marshall Klaus, one of her former colleagues at Stanford Medical School. Klaus, who was chief of the intensive care nursery, conducted an experiment in which half the babies in the nursery would be treated as usual, that is to say with high-tech incubators and millions of dollars of equipment, and the other half would be touched for fifteen minutes every few hours. Nurses would simply take their "pinky" finger and gently rub it down the backs of these tiny infants. This was out of the ordinary as these intensive care babies were not often touched for fear of getting germs on them. The results were astounding. They discovered that the babies who were touched survived better. Dr. Remen said, "No one knows why. Maybe there's something about touching that strengthens the will to live. Maybe isolation weakens us."[2]

Indeed it does. We were not created for isolation. We were created for community—with God and with one another. Community is at the core of who we are and who God is.

GOD SEEKS COMMUNITY

The Bible is the story of God pursuing and enjoying relationships. God seeks out Adam and Eve in the Garden. He engages them. He asks them, "Where are you?" God invites Abraham to be in a covenant relationship. God wrestles with Jacob. God converses on a mountaintop with Moses. God binds himself/herself to the people of Israel. God speaks to Elijah in a still, small voice. Then in the fullness of time, God comes to us in the form of a human—Jesus—that we might know him/her better. The God-man Jesus says to his disciples, "I do not call you servants any longer . . . but I have called you friends" (John 16:15).

The entire Bible tells the story of God reaching out to us, pursuing us, even to the point of becoming one of us.

In his book *All I Really Need to Know I Learned in Kindergarten*, Robert Fulghum tells of playing two games as a child, "Hide-and-seek" and "Sardines." It is too bad I missed the game "Sardines" as a child because it sounds like fun. In Sardines, the person who is "it" goes and hides, and everybody starts looking. When you find the person, you join in the hiding. Pretty soon everybody is giggling and laughing and hiding together. Fulghum makes this observation: "Medieval theologians even described God in hide-and-seek terms, calling him *Deus Absconditus*. But me, I think old God is a Sardine player and will be found the same way everybody gets found in Sardines—by the sound of laughter of those heaped together at the end."[3]

God enjoys getting close to people. One of God's names is "Emmanuel": God with us. God is not far way. God comes near. God seeks us out.

GOD MODELS COMMUNITY

God not only seeks but also MODELS community for us. We see it modeled in the very personhood of God. Of all the things we say about God, one of the clearest is that God is three persons, the Trinity. We sing:

> Holy, holy, holy! Lord God Almighty!
>   All Thy works shall praise Thy name
>   in earth and sky and sea;
> Holy, holy, holy! merciful and mighty!
>   God in three persons, blessed Trinity![4]

Of course, we are not always sure what we are saying when we sing, "Blessed Trinity." We may not understand the "Blessed Trinity" any better than little Natalie. When talking to her about God, Natalie's father asked her a trick question. He asked, "Of the Father, Son, and Holy Spirit, which of them is God?"

Four-year-old Natalie answered, "The tallest one."

The Trinity is a mystery to most of us. The question of how God can be One in Three and Three in One at the same time boggles our minds and has kept theologians busy for years. In attempting to explain the mystery, we have turned to such images as God being like an egg (yoke, white, and shell) or the three forms of water (ice, liquid, and steam) or as a man who can be a son, husband, and father all at the same time or a woman who can be a daughter, a wife, and a mother all at the same time. All these images fall short, however, of fully capturing the doctrine of the Trinity. Our finite minds cannot get around this infinite mystery. We do not understand how it all works. We do not comprehend how God can be three distinct and knowable persons, but still One. What we can say with some certainty, however, is that God is a divine being in community with himself/herself. Gareth Icenogle has even gone so far as to refer to God as a self-contained small group, and rightly so. He says, "It may be overly dramatic to say that God lives as a *small group,* but the church has historically described God as Trinity, three persons in one . . . God is described as existing in divine community, in dialogue with other members of the God-self."[5]

This communal nature of the Godhead may be one of the most important affirmations we can make about God. It certainly has profound implications when we consider the image of God that has been passed on to humankind. As God is a being living in a mutually interdependent community, so we humans are beings created for community. We have been given a "communal gene" by our Creator. We have been designed and imprinted for relationships.

We see community not only modeled *in* the Godhead, but also *by* the God-man, Jesus. Reading the Gospels, one gets the impression that Jesus spends as much time in community with his disciples as he does preaching the Good News. The Gospel writer Mark gives us a great insight into this when he writes, "And he appointed twelve, whom he called apostles, to be with him" (Mark 3:14).

Jesus invited people to be *with* him. Jesus did not just minister *to* or *at* people. Jesus ministered *with* people. If anyone could have made it on his own, not needing others, it would appear to have been Jesus. He was divine. He could have gotten things done without getting involved with messy humans, yet he did not do that. He called others to be with him. He modeled the importance of community.

There is a wonderful story about Jimmy Durante, one of the great entertainers of a generation ago. Durante had been asked to be a part of a show for World War II veterans. In response to the request to perform, he told the organizers that his schedule was very busy and that he could afford only a few minutes, but if they would not mind his doing one short monologue and his leaving immediately for his next appointment, he would come. Of course, the show's director happily agreed to those conditions.

When Durante got on stage, however, something interesting happened. He went through his short monologue, and then he stayed. As he entertained, the applause grew louder and louder, and he kept at it. Pretty soon he had been on stage for fifteen, then twenty, then thirty minutes. Finally, he took his last bow and left the stage. Backstage, someone stopped him and said, "I thought you had to go after a few minutes. What happened?"

Durante answered, "I did have to go, but I can show you the reason I stayed. You can see for yourself if you will look down on the front row."

In the front row were two men, each of whom had lost an arm in the war. One had lost his right arm and the other had lost his left. Together, they were able to clap, and that is exactly what they were doing loudly and cheerfully—clapping.

Scripture makes it clear that we really do need one another. Right from the start, on page two of the Bible, God says, "It is not good that the man should be alone" (Genesis 2:18), and later we see Jesus model this very thing by calling the Twelve to be with him.

GOD BUILDS COMMUNITY

God not only enjoys community and models community, God also BUILDS community.

Surely there is no encounter between two people more famous or more anticipated than the meeting of Adam and Eve. It had been a tiring and disappointing day for Adam. He had spent the day naming all the animals, every beast of the field and every bird of the air. Snakes, lizards, eagles, lions, rhinos, tarantulas, pigeons, seals, and swordfish, he named them all. Then there was no one or no thing left to name, and he was still lonely. There was no one in the garden like him. Exhausted from the day's work, Adam drifted off to sleep, and when he awoke, he noticed he was missing a rib. He also noticed something else, something he called a woman. At last he had what he had been missing. He had community with another like himself. In this story God bestows upon Adam and Eve the most intimate of all human communities, the community of marriage.

I have a daughter in college. In a few years I look forward to being something I have never been before: the father of the bride. As a pastor I have performed hundreds of weddings, but I have never been the father of the bride. In this story, God becomes the father of the bride.[6] God presents Eve to Adam. God builds the first human community.

God did not stop with Adam and Eve. After their banishment from the garden, God went on to build a larger community. The Creator built a covenant community. Covenants were common in the ancient Near East. They served as contracts or formal agreements between two parties, usually between two kings or between a king and his subjects. When a person entered into a covenant agreement, he/she entered into a binding relationship with the other person.

Reading the Old Testament, we encounter a community-building, covenanting God. The two first covenants recorded in the Bible chronicle God's covenants with Noah. In the first covenant (Genesis 6:18), God promises to save Noah and his family if Noah would build an Ark and bring every living creature into it. In the second covenant (Genesis 9:9), God promises Noah and his descendants never again to destroy the earth by flood.

Years later God makes another covenant. This time God enters into a binding relationship with Abraham. In this covenant God promises to build a nation, a covenant community of people, as numerous as the stars in the sky:

> The Lord appeared to Abram, and said to him, "I am God Almighty, walk before me and be blameless. And I will make my covenant between me and you, and will make you exceedingly numerous ... I will make you exceedingly fruitful; and I will make nations of you, and kings shall come from you. I will establish my covenant between me and you, and your offspring after you throughout their generations, for an everlasting covenant, to be God to you and to your offspring after you." (Genesis 17:1-2; 6-7)

Centuries later, this dream becomes a reality. The covenant community conceived in Abraham is born at Sinai. The rest of the Old Testament records God's interaction with this community. God gives laws to order it, calls kings to lead it, prophets to correct it, and other nations to discipline it. When those efforts fall on deaf ears and land on stubborn hearts, God proceeds to build another community, the Church.

Jesus' words ring in our ears: "Upon this rock I will build my church, and the gates of Hades will not prevail against it" (Matthew

16:13). Jesus' disciple Peter does not have many shining moments, but he has one when he responds to the question, "Who do you say that I am?" with, "You are the Messiah, the Son of the Living God" (Matthew 16:16).

Elsewhere in the Scriptures we see Jesus laugh; we see him cry; we see him angry. Here, after hearing Peter's affirmation of faith, Jesus is filled with joy. He is getting through to the disciples. Peter understands who he is. All Jesus' teaching and preaching and miracle working come together in this synergistic moment of insight for Peter.

The Greek word for church is *ekklesia*. The word literally means, "the called out ones," but this definition raises a question—called out for what? For service? Yes. For sacrifice? Yes. For mission? Yes. For community? Most emphatically!

The word *ekklesia* appears one-hundred-twelve times in the New Testament and is used primarily to designate a communal reality.[7] The *ekklesia* is the people of God (2 Corinthians 6:16), the new humanity (Revelation 14:4), the household and family (Matthew 10:6), the saints and servants (2 Corinthians 4:5). The *ekklesia* is not a building, nor a religious institution, but is the company of the committed where we are brothers and sisters in fellowship with Christ and one another. The Apostle Paul likens the *ekklesia* to a human body. He writes,

> Indeed, the body does not consist of one member but of many. If the foot would say, "Because I am not a hand, I do not belong to the body," that would not make it any less a part of the body. And if the ear would say, "Because I am not an eye, I do not belong to the body," that would not make it any less a part of the body. If the whole body were an eye, where would the hearing be? If the whole body were hearing, where would the sense of smell be? But as it is, God arranged the members in the body, each one of them, as he chose. God has so arranged the body . . . that there be no dissension within the body, but the members may have the same care for one another. (1 Corinthians 12:14-18; 24-25)

I can remember Thanksgiving 1981 as if it were yesterday. I was in Brookings, Oregon, pastoring a small Presbyterian congregation. After morning worship we returned home, set up a card table in the living room, and proceeded to put together a thousand-piece jigsaw puzzle. It took us four days to do it. It was a labor of love, finding each piece and putting it in the proper place.

God builds the church in a similar manner. God gives members of the *ekklesia* special talents and special gifts and then carefully fits them together with patience, love, and care.

GOD COMMANDS COMMUNITY

Of course, God not only enjoys community, models community, and builds community, but also God COMMANDS community. In his farewell address Jesus gathers his disciples together and says, "I give you a new commandment, that you love one another. Just as I have loved you, you also should love one another. By this everyone will know that you are my disciples, if you have love for one another" (John 13:34-35).

How, then, are members of the *ekklesia* to love one another? As Jesus did: Sacrificially. Selflessly. Understandingly. Forgivingly. Members of the *ekklesia* make sacrifices for one another. They give in to one another. They go out of their way for one another. Members of the *ekklesia* think of others, not just themselves. Members of the *ekklesia* take time to get to know one another. They invest themselves in one another. They put one another on their calendars. Members of the *ekklesia* also forgive one another. Ponder the words of Bill Hybels, pastor of one of the largest Reformed congregations in the United States:

> *Unity* isn't the word we use to describe relationships at Willow Creek. The popular concept of unity is a fantasy land where disagreements never surface and contrary opinions are never stated with force. We expect disagreement, forceful disagreement. So instead of unity, we use the word *community*. The mark of community—true biblical unity—is *not* the absence of conflict. It's the presence of a reconciling spirit.[8]

The Community of Christ is a place where people of opposite quarters, like Simon the political activist, and Matthew the tax collector, learn to love one another. In the Community of Christ people of extremes meet—tax haters and tax collectors, gays and straights, pro-lifers and pro-choicers—and work to find common ground because Jesus commands it.

This command to love one another, however, is just one of *fifty-one* "one another" commands in the Bible. In addition to the fourteen "love one anothers," we are commanded to fashion a community of kindness, forgiveness, hospitality, humbleness, service, instruction, exhortation, prayer, submission, and harmony. The Greek word for it is *koinonia*. We translate the word into English as "fellowship," but fellowship does not do the term justice. *Koinonia* involves both a horizontal and a vertical connection. It is an in-depth, simultaneous connection with Christ and one another. It is Christ's promise to be present whenever two or three are gathered in his name.

GOD SENDS US OUT IN COMMUNITY

Finally, God not only enjoys, models, builds, and commands community but also SENDS people into the world in community.

Jesus appointed seventy others and sent them on ahead of him in pairs to every town and place where he himself intended to go. He said to them, "Whenever you enter a town and its people welcome you, eat what is set before you; cure the sick who are there, and say to them, 'The kingdom of God has come near to you.' But whenever you enter a town and they do not welcome you, go out into its streets and say, 'Even the dust of your town that clings to our feet, we wipe off in protest against you. Yet know this: the kingdom of God has come near.' I tell you, on that day it will be more tolerable for Sodom than for that town (Luke 10:8-12). Assignments do not get much tougher than this. The seventy faced the probability of rejection.

The most remarkable thing Jesus did to prepare the seventy for their ministry was to send them out in pairs. He put into operation a spiritual "buddy system" so they could look out for one another. Sam Shoemaker, the Episcopal priest who helped found Alcoholics Anonymous and Faith At Work, summed up the Christian life in three short sentences: Get changed. Get together. Get going.

There is a spiritual energy released when two or more get going together. Teaming together produces powerful results. As the author of Ecclesiastes states, "Two are better than one because they have a good reward for their toil" (Ecclesiastes 4:9). We see this power of community in the animal kingdom. In a horse pull in Canada, one horse pulled nine thousand pounds. Another horse pulled eight thousand pounds. Together one would expect them to pull seventeen thousand pounds, but that is not the case. When yoked together, those two horses pulled thirty thousand pounds. Geese provide another example. Geese fly in a "V" formation because the flapping action of their wings creates an upward lift for the goose that follows. This action gives the entire flock a seventy-one percent greater range than if each bird flew alone.

Without a teammate alongside praying, encouraging, bearing burdens, we will never be as effective as we can be. We were imprinted for community, and we function powerfully in community.

YOUR COMMUNITY

Robert Wuthrow, Professor of Social Sciences and Director of the Center for the Study of American Religion at Princeton University, writes:

> Nearly everyone in our society desperately wants community, but . . . most people have trouble finding it in all the ways they would like it to be present in their lives. Neighborhoods and the workplace provide opportunities for interaction, but for most people these arenas do not yield the sharing and caring they desire. Small groups are the alternative.[9]

Indeed, they are. That is why so many Americans (four out of ten) belong to one. In small groups (a gathering of three to twelve people who meet together on a regular basis for support and encouragement), people move beyond interaction to community. They find in small groups a place where they can bring their lives—their hopes, dreams, doubts, frustrations, and joys—and share them with one another.

In the chapters that follow, you will be given the opportunity to do the very same thing. You are invited to bring your life to others in your group as you study ten of the "one another" passages from the Bible. May you experience the joy of small group community as you open yourself to God and one another.

CHAPTER TWO

MEET TOGETHER

*And let us consider how to provoke one another to love
and good works, not neglecting to meet together,
as is the habit of some.*
Hebrews 10:24, 25

GETTING STARTED

I was sitting in "Angels" restaurant with four other people. This was
the first time our breakfast group was meeting, and our intent was to
become a small group. After we ordered our cereal and eggs and toast,
we asked each other to respond to four questions as a way of getting to
know one another. The questions were easy to answer. Try them with
your group. Take one question at a time. Be brief and to the point. After
everyone has shared, go to the next question.

> • QUESTION 1: *"Share your name and place of birth."*
> I answered the question with these words: "I was born in Hilo,
Hawaii. My mother was born and raised in Hilo. My father met my
mother during the Second World War. He was in the Marine Corps.
Though born in Hawaii, I was raised in southern California. My
mother gave birth to me when she was twenty years old."

> • QUESTION 2: *"Give us a quick glimpse of your current
> family situation."*
> I answered, "My wife, Trudy, and I have been married twenty-
six years. We have two children. Joshua, age twenty-three, recently
graduated from the University of Kansas. He is working for a "Big Six"
accounting firm in Kansas City, Missouri. Jennifer, age twenty, is a junior at Florida State University. She was recently elected president of
her sorority, and she is a public relations major. For the most part,
Trudy and I are now 'empty nesters' and we greatly enjoy this stage of

life. When Jennifer gets out of school, we will no longer be suffering from maltuition!"

- QUESTION 3: *"Name a couple of things that have put a smile on your face recently."*

I shared, "One thing that pops into my mind is that my wife just got a new job. She recently returned to the world of real estate and is managing a residential real estate office near our home. You should see her. She loves what she is doing. There is added spring to her step. The other thing that has me smiling is being with you in this group. I have been looking forward to this gathering for the past month. I hope the group becomes what I know it can become."

- QUESTION 4: *"When did God begin to become more than just a word to you?"*

I responded, "Back in college when I was volunteering at a YMCA in Glendale, California. The Glendale YMCA was one of those rare YMCA's that still took the 'Christ' in Young Men's Christian Association seriously. Most YMCAs are health clubs and family centers, not places to discover God. The Glendale 'Y' was different. In fact, the Glendale 'Y' even hired nearby seminary students to staff many of their children- and youth-programs.

"I became involved with the 'Y' when a friend, Hank Giardina, recruited me to coach a fourth grade boys' football team. While at the 'Y' I met a number of young men who loved sports—and God. That combination was new to me. Most of my models of faith were women, not men, and certainly not any men who loved sports. After a year of volunteering and spending time with the 'Y' staff, I ended up giving all I knew of myself to all I knew of God. All this took place when I was a freshman at UCLA."

THE GROUND RULES

Like my breakfast group, this may be the first time your small group has met. As a result, you may have all sorts of questions about being in a group. You may be asking yourself, "What will be expected of me? What if I do not like the group? What if they do not like me? What if the leader asks me to share things I would rather not share? How long am I expected to stay in this group?" Then again, you may be in a group that has been meeting for months or even years. You may be quite comfortable with small group life and have found intentional Christian community to be an important discipline on your spiritual journey. Whether you are a small group rookie or small group veteran, four ground rules need to be observed. Take time in your group to look over, discuss, and commit to these four rules:

- Confidentiality: What is shared in the group, stays in the group.
- Attendance: Everyone makes attending group gatherings a high priority.
- No Advice Giving: Group members are to "care," not "cure." Group members refrain from "fixing the problem." Instead, they help "bear the burden." Advice is offered only when requested.
- Participation: Group members have the right to their own opinions. Questions will be encouraged and respected. Everyone has permission to pass. No one will be asked to share what they do not want to share.

What, if any, ground rules would you like to add to this list?

Your group will also need to consider how often you intend to meet together as a group. Will you meet weekly, every other week, twice a month, monthly? The regularity of your meeting together will have significant implications for the health and vitality of your group. Generally speaking, the more often a group meets the more successfully the group will meet the intimacy needs of its members. For example, if a person joins a group that meets weekly and she has to be out of town on a business trip once during the month, she will still meet three times with her group members that month. If, however, she is in a group that only meets twice a month, and she has to miss a meeting, she will only meet one time that month with the members of her group. If she is in a monthly group and is out of town or ill, she misses the group entirely that month.

Most groups need to meet at least twice a month in order for members to stay current with each other. Less than that, it is difficult for group members to stay up to date with what is happening in one another's lives. The Bible has something to say about the importance of meeting together. In the Book of Hebrews we read,

Let us hold fast to the confession of our hope without wavering, for he who has promised is faithful. And let us consider how to provoke one another to love and good works, *not neglecting to meet together, as is the habit of some [italics mine]*, but encouraging one another, and all the more as you see the Day approaching. (Hebrews 10:23-25)

Someone called the Book of Hebrews the "riddle" of the New Testament.[1] By that he meant we are left to guess and grope about the author, the recipients, and the date of the book. Who wrote this letter? Paul? Barnabas? Priscilla? Where did the recipients of the letter live? Jerusalem? Ephesus? Rome? When was it written? 65 A.D.? 80 A.D.? 90 A.D.? We do not know. We are left to fill in the blanks.

Despite these mysteries, however, some things we can know with great certainty. For example, we know the Book of Hebrews was written to a church that had been meeting for a long period of time. The author writes, "For though by this time you ought to have been teachers, you need someone to teach you again the basic elements of the oracles of God" (Hebrews 5:12). We also know that this particular church had suffered through some very tough times: "Recall those earlier days when, after you had been enlightened, you endured a hard struggle with sufferings, sometimes being publicly exposed to abuse and persecuted" (Hebrews 10:32-33). Moreover, we know some members of this church had stopped meeting together. In fact, *not* meeting had become a bad spiritual habit in their lives.

Why these members neglected meeting together we can only guess. Maybe they got out of the habit of meeting during a time of great persecution. Maybe they thought they could make it on their own without the support of Christian brothers and sisters. Maybe they feared renewed persecution from Roman authorities if they were seen congregating together in the name of Christ.

BENEFITS OF MEETING TOGETHER

Whatever the reason, we get the sense that the author of Hebrews deeply believed that meeting together was critical to keeping one's faith alive. He said meeting together helps us to hold fast to our confession of hope (Hebrews 10:23). It helps us to abound in love and good works (Hebrews 10:24), and it builds our courage in uncertain times (Hebrews 10:25).

Reading what the author of Hebrews writes, I think of my camping days with the YMCA. As is the case with most camps, we had a campfire each night and the task of one of the cabin groups each evening was to put out the fire. When it was my cabin's turn to put it out, we were told to do two things. First, we were to douse the fire with water, making sure we soaked the logs. Then we were instructed to separate the logs because, even though they were wet, any logs still touching each other had a good chance of reigniting.

This "separation" principle applies to relationships. I think of a husband and wife who, just before Christmas, went to a jewelry store to look for an opal ring for their daughter. The daughter had wanted an October birth stone ring, but when the mother and father looked at all the different birth stones, all were more spectacular than the opal. Compared to the other stones, the opal looked drab. When the father mentioned this to the clerk, she said, "Watch this." Then she took one of the opal rings and began to rub the stone in the palm of her hand. She said as she rubbed, "These rings have been sitting a long time, and just need a touch of warmth." About thirty seconds later, the clerk held out the ring for the family to see. It gleamed and flashed all the colors of the rainbow. It was beautiful. The family bought it and the daughter loves it.

Similarly, without the touch and warmth of other human beings, the spark can go out of our lives. Our faith can become dull and colorless. We can lose hope and become easily discouraged. Meeting together keeps that from happening. The author of Ecclesiastes put it this way:

> Two are better than one, because they have a good reward for their toil. For if they fall, one will lift up the other; but woe to one who is alone and falls and does not have another to help. Again, if two lie together, they keep warm; but how can one keep warm alone? And though one might prevail against another, two will withstand one. A threefold cord is not quickly broken. (Ecclesiastes 4:9-12)

Given all the benefits of meeting together, why do so many choose not to do it? Even though four out of every ten Americans currently choose to be in a small group, that still leaves six out of ten not in a group. What keeps them from meeting together in order to offer mutual support and encouragement?

BARRIERS TO MEETING TOGETHER

The most obvious reason is IGNORANCE. Most people do not know how much being in a small group can mean to them. I think of three men whose wives dragged them to their first small group meeting. They came only because they knew the leader of the group, Charlie Scott. If Charlie had not been leading the group, these men would never have come to that first meeting. Charlie was a "guy's-guy." He played basketball at the University of Tennessee. He was ordained in the Presbyterian Church and, with his wife, Mary, he coordinated the church-partnership division of Young Life.

Charlie and Mary also started a couples' small group in our congregation. They invited some of their friends to join them. They asked their friends to give it four weeks and if they did not like it, they could gracefully drop out of the group. The husbands came only because Charlie was there and because they could quit after four meetings. They all intended to drop out after the first four sessions, convinced being in a small group was not for them. A year has passed, and those husbands are still in the group. In fact, they now lead studies and close the group in prayer from time to time.

What changed? They moved from ignorance to awareness. They realized what a small group could do for themselves and their marriages. They now say things like, " I never knew what I was missing!" and "I would recommend being in a group to anyone."

After discovering the joy of small group life, others have said:

"My small group means a place where Christian friends meet and where I know I will be accepted as I am. It is a time during a busy and hectic week when I can take a deep breath, relax and face the rest of the week." —*Middle-Age Woman*

"I hate to miss our group. I feel so much better after the meeting."—*Single, Young Man*

"It is one place where I can be what I am, and know that my concerns are being prayed for by others who care. It is also a place where I can understand a discussion of the Gospel with other Christians in an open, understanding atmosphere."—*Thirty-Something Father*

"For me a covenant group has been a group of Christian friends who constantly show me that I am loved and accepted even when I don't feel that way. But what excites me even more is that my small group challenges me to grow in my faith as I study and learn with them and pray for them."—*Twenty-Something Mother*

"Since the arrival of my grandchildren, the most wonderful thing to happen to me has been my small group. My Christian maturity has grown more in the past few months with the help of this group than in all the rest of my life. Miracles are happening, prayers are answered, faith is deepening, life is more worth living because of this wonderful group of people."—*A Grandfather*

* * *

A second reason the majority of Americans are not in a small group has to do with TIME. We just do not have enough of it. Attempting to fit another meeting, another commitment into an already packed schedule seems impossible. I think of the Japanese artist who painted a picture on a fairly large canvas. Down in one corner was a tree, and on the limbs of the tree were some birds—but all the rest of the canvas was bare. When asked if he were going to paint something more to fill the rest of the canvas, he said, "Oh no, I have to leave room for the birds to fly."

Emergency bypass surgery at the age of forty-eight caused me to re-evaluate my canvas. My life was so packed with meetings and agendas and commitments, I had little room to fly. I felt like my wings had been clipped. Then I went to the doctor for what I thought was bursitis in my shoulder, only to be told I had coronary artery disease and surgery was necessary. Six weeks of convalescing after a double-bypass helped me put things into perspective. What I thought was once so very important was no longer significant, and what I had taken for granted suddenly became momentous. Over time, I have left more room on my canvas for those things that cause me to soar. One of those things has been my small group. An associate of the Covey Leadership Center put it well:

> I attended a seminar once where the instructor was lecturing on time. At one point, he said, "Okay, it's time for a quiz." He reached under the table and pulled out a wide-mouth gallon jar. He set it on the table next to a platter with some fist-sized rocks on it. "How many of these rocks do you think we can get in the jar?" he asked.
>
> After we made our guess, he said, "Okay. Let's find out." He set one rock in the jar . . . then another . . . then another. I don't remember how many he got in, but he got the jar full. Then he asked, "Is that jar full?"
>
> Everybody looked at the rocks and said, "Yes."
>
> Then he said, "Ahhh." He reached under the table and pulled out a bucket of gravel. Then he dumped some gravel in and shook the jar and the gravel went in all the little spaces left by the big rocks. Then he grinned and said once more, "Is the jar full?"
>
> By this time we were on to him. "Probably not," we said.
>
> "Good!" he replied. And he reached under the table and brought out a bucket of sand. He started dumping the sand in and it went in all the little spaces left by the rocks and the gravel. Once more he looked at us and said, "Is the jar full?"
>
> "No!" we all roared.
>
> He said, "Good!" and he grabbed a pitcher of water and began to pour it in. He got something like a quart of water in that jar.
>
> Then he said, "Well, what's the point?"
>
> Somebody said, "Well, there are gaps, and if you really work at it, you can always fit more into your life."
>
> "No," he said, "that's not the point. The point is this: if you hadn't put these big rocks in first, would you ever have gotten any of them in?"[2]

Being in a small group has become a "big rock" for me. I make sure it "gets into my jar" right after time with God, myself, my family. I benefit greatly from the accountability, encouragement, and support I receive from my group.

* * *

There is a third major barrier to meeting together: FEAR. We have to overcome three trepidations before joining a group. The first is the fear of self-disclosure. Most of us fear being asked to share more than we are comfortable sharing. We do not want to be put on the spot. When we join a group we want some guarantees that we will be asked to reveal only what we feel comfortable revealing about ourselves.

I remember a horrible time when I attended a renewal conference. I still get shivers thinking about it. The speaker's opening message was humorous, entertaining, and insightful. He talked about family systems. What he said made sense. I thought about my family of origin and the roles we had all assumed. I was glad I had decided to come. Then the speaker asked us to form a group of three. I did so willingly. After all, I liked meeting new people. Then he dropped the bomb. He said, "Share, with the people in your group, your family's secret." Well, that was more than I wanted to tell these strangers. I felt trapped. I felt angry that he would ask us to share something so personal with people we had just met. If this had been my first experience with a small group, I likely would have not given small groups another chance!

To make sure something similar does not happen in your group, do two things. First, give one another "permission to pass." If anyone in the group ever feels uncomfortable answering a question, give them permission not to answer. When it is their turn to share, they can simply say, "I pass." Second, attempt to match the level of sharing questions to the level of the group. The more time we spend together, the more comfortable we become sharing the raw material of our lives with one another. The sharing questions for new groups will be quite different from the sharing questions for groups who have more history together.

It is like learning how to swim. There is one method of learning aquatics I do not recommend: having someone throw us into the deep end of the pool and see how we do. We might make it safely to the other side of the pool, but we will not appreciate the experience. A better method is more systematic. First, we learn how to kick our feet and legs in the water. Then, we learn how to use our arms. Next, comes how to breathe while swimming. After mastering these basics, we start by swimming across the shallow end of the pool. That way, if something goes wrong, we can easily touch the bottom of the pool. When we can confidently swim in the shallow end, then we can move into deeper waters.

The same principle applies to sharing questions in a group. We begin in shallow waters and, when we become more confident with one another, we move into deeper waters.

* * *

There is another fear that people have about small groups in the church: We do not want others to know how little we know about the Bible. That certainly was the case for me. When I began seminary, I did not know much about the Bible. In fact, I remember my embarrassment when professors asked us to turn to a certain book of the Bible. At the time, outside of the four Gospels, I did not know which books were in the New Testament and which were in the Old Testament! To cover my embarrassment, I always kept one finger in the table of contents at the beginning of the Bible. That way when a professor asked us to turn to a book of the Bible such as Nahum or Ezra, I could scan the contents, find the page number of the book, and turn to it as quickly as possible.

Many people in small groups feel like I did back in seminary. They want to study the Bible but they are embarrassed by their lack of knowledge about it—so much so that they might hesitate to join a group. They do not want that secret to be known by others, especially if they have been in the church for years.

Years ago, I was asked to write some discussion questions for the *Serendipity Bible for Groups*.[3] (The *Serendipity Bible for Groups* contains small group sharing and discussion questions in the margins for every book of the Bible.) The project coordinator, Dietrich Gruen, did not want to scare people off with questions that might expose someone's lack of biblical knowledge. His goal was to provide sharing questions that presupposed little or no previous biblical knowledge so that group members would sense they were on the same ground. These were his instructions to me:

> Imagine a group like this: In the group you have 'Bible Billy' and Bible Bertha.' They have not missed a Sunday School class in twenty-six years. Their Sunday School class is currently studying Paul's Letter to the Philippians. They have been studying it for three years! Then

there is 'Biker Bob.' He has never read the Bible. He is not a Christian. He is searching for something in his life, visited the church, heard about small groups and signed up. The rest of the group resides somewhere in between those two extremes. Write questions that do not insult 'Bible Billy' and 'Bible Bertha,' that interest the rest of the group, and yet do not scare off 'Biker Bob.'

I have tried to do that in this book. If you are a serious student of the Scriptures, I hope you will be challenged by the questions posed in this book. On the other hand, if you are new to groups and new to studying the Bible, I hope you will find this experience well within your comfort zone.

* * *

The final fear of small groups in the church relates to prayer—specifically, the fear of being asked to pray out loud in front of others. In fact, the number one fear of Americans is the fear of public speaking. Praying out loud in a group taps into that fear. Granted, when we pray we are speaking to God, but others are listening to the conversation, and we do not want to say anything that would embarrass us. Then, to complicate matters, such prayers often become a spirituality measuring stick. That is to say, if one can speak eloquent verbal prayers, he or she must be a spiritual giant. If one stumbles with words when praying, that person must be a spiritual pygmy. We do not want to appear like a spiritual lightweight, so we shy away from situations where we might be asked to pray out loud.

Because of this fear, I encourage your group to move slowly when it comes to prayer. You might want to begin with silent prayer for one another. Simply take a minute of silence at the end of the group to picture the faces of everyone and thank God for them. A few sessions later you might progress to "popcorn" prayer. This involves saying words or phrases that pop into one's mind when a subject or a person is mentioned in prayer. In "popcorn" prayer the leader begins by saying, "God we thank you for . . . " and leaves the sentenced open-ended. Group members complete the sentence by offering words of thanksgiving, such as . . . friendships . . . job interviews . . . successful surgery . . . Jan's friendship. After thanksgiving, the leader may say, "And God we bring before you . . . ," again leaving the sentence open-ended. Group members can complete the sentence in words or very short phrases. This style of prayer enables people to learn to pray with others without having to compose eloquent sentences.

Later, after the group is together for a while, the group may be ready to pray for the person on one's left or right. This can be done in silence, or it can be done briefly with three or four simple sentences, thanking God for that person and praying for that person's prayer request. However your group decides to handle your prayer time, recognize the fact that not everyone in the group will be at the same comfort level with praying out loud. Remember to move slowly and sensitively in this area of meeting together.

Choosing to be in this group shows you have overcome some of these fears, or at least are willing to face them. I affirm your courage and assure you that this book is written with those fears in mind.

GROUP DISCUSSION AND SHARING

1. **Getting to Know One Another** *(20-30 minutes)*
    - If you haven't done so already, share your answers to the four questions on pages 27 and 28.

2. **Discussion** *(10-15 minutes)*
    - What comments would you like to make about the material in the chapter?

3. **Group Sharing Questions** *(15-20 minutes)*
    Go around the circle and give each person time to answer the first question before going on to the next question.

    - Why did you decide to come to this group?
      ___ I could not come up with an excuse to get out of it.
      ___ I was curious about what a small group is like.
      ___ Someone important to me said, "Come or else!"
      ___ It is something I have wanted to do for a long time.
      ___ Someone invited me.
      ___ I heard about it and thought I would give it a try.
      ___ Other.

- What do you hope to get out of the group?
___ I hope to learn more about myself.
___ I hope to learn more about the Bible.
___ I hope to make some good friends.
___ I hope to grow closer to God.
___ I hope to feel more connected to the church.
___ I hope to learn how to love others more deeply.
___ I want to understand different perspectives on faith and religion.
___ Other.

- What fears do you have about being in the group?
___ I will be asked to share something I feel uncomfortable sharing.
___ People will discover how little I know about the Bible.
___ Someone will ask me to pray out loud.
___ I will be trapped and unable to get out of the group if I do not like it.
___ People in the group will not like me.
___ I will not like the people in the group.
___ I will do something to embarrass myself.
___ Someone in the group will break confidentiality.
___ Other.

4. **Sharing Prayer Concerns and Prayer** (*15-20 minutes*)
- How would you like the group to be praying for you in the coming week?
- Close in silent prayer. While praying, picture the face of each person in your group and thank God for him or her.

CHAPTER THREE

ACCEPT ONE ANOTHER

Accept one another, then,
just as Christ accepted you,
in order to bring praise to God.
Romans 15:7 NIV

Small group guru Dale Galloway relates a wonderful story about a spunky little orphan boy and his remarkable church:

> On a cold, windy morning in Chicago with the wind-chill factor well below zero, the orphan boy, Ralph, walked four miles to church. His friend, Mr. Kennedy, greeted him as he came in the door, "Glad to see you, Ralph. Sure is cold out there today."
>
> With a smile Ralph said, "I sure did get cold walking this morning."
>
> Surprised, the older man inquired, "You mean you walked here to church this morning?"
>
> Ralph replied, "Yep, I didn't have money for bus fare."
>
> "Well, how far did you walk, Ralph?"
>
> "I walked four miles."
>
> Mr. Kennedy asked Ralph, "How many churches did you pass along the way walking four miles?"
>
> Ralph thought for a moment. "I passed twenty-two churches."
>
> Impressed, Mr. Kennedy said, "Ralph, why did you pass all those churches just to come to our church on this cold morning?
>
> Ralph smiled widely and said, "Because I've discovered that here they love a fella like me.[1]

Young and old, rich and poor, male and female will walk, run, and drive miles to pockets of community where they find love and acceptance. Why? Because these communities provide an oasis in a world of "put downs." Bruce Larson said it well:

> One of the sad things about life on this globe is that so many people are trying to put other people down. Some of my most painful memories come from my own childhood experiences or from watching children minimize, humiliate, and shame one another. Anyone who is different, deformed, unlovely, or awkward has no shortage of people to point that out to him. As we get older it seems we are still quick to point out another's failures. We may not be as overtly cruel, but we are quick to make those around us feel stupid or inferior.[2]

My hands still become clammy when I think back to my junior high days. I was different. I lived on the wrong side of the tracks. In elementary school I had been king: Student Body President, President of the LetterMens' Club. Other kids wanted to be my friend and sit next to me at lunch. Then, in the middle of the sixth grade, we moved across town. My parents thought by moving I would be attending a better junior high. Academically, the school may have been better, but relationally, it was a nightmare. It was the worst move of my life.

The worst part was having to ride the bus to school. Only kids who lived on the "wrong" side of the tracks rode the bus to school. They were poorer, they did not dress "right," and the more affluent kids in school made fun of them. After a month of riding the bus, I did whatever I could to avoid it. I begged my mother to drive me to school. I rode my bike when it did not rain. Then, on those days when I could not avoid the bus, I made sure as few people as possible saw me. I waited until everyone else had gotten off the bus to sneak off. At the end of the day, I waited until the last possible minute to get on. I boarded swiftly, quickly finding a seat and slumping down so no one could see me. After being "in" in elementary school, I was "out" in junior high.

A MODEL FOR ACCEPTANCE

It is horrible feeling that you are on the "outside." The pain can be excruciating. I think of the story of the Samaritan woman whom Jesus encountered on his way from Judea to Galilee (John 4:1-42). The most direct way to get from Judea in the south to Galilee in the north was through Samaria. While making such a trip, Jesus came to the Samaritan town of Sychar and stopped at a spot that would have been listed in a AAA Tourbook if they had such things in those days. Jacob's well was an historical site that had many Jewish memories attached to it, dating back to Old Testament days of Jacob and Joseph.

Jesus and his band arrived at the well midday when the heat would have been the greatest. Tired from the journey, Jesus sent his disciples into town to purchase food. Usually no one came for water in the middle of the day, but shortly after he got comfortable, a woman arrived with a heavy jar on her shoulder. Jesus had only to look at her to know the story. Only "outcasts" came at this hour. The "respectable" women in town would come in the evening when the temperatures were cooler. These evening gatherings at the well were sort of a social institution where women in the village came to exchange small talk and learn the latest village news. This woman who came at noon side-stepped all that to avoid the pain and embarrassment of being ostracized, the object of village gossip.

Her sin? Loose living. She had been married five times and was living with someone new. Jesus surprised her when he asked for a drink. After all, Jews did not share things in common with Samaritans—something akin to separate drinking fountains for blacks and whites in the early part of the twentieth century in the United States. Not only that, Jesus must have known something was up, considering the type of woman who would come to the well at noon. But speak Jesus did, and they had quite a conversation. They talked about all sorts of things: worship, Jews and Samaritans, holy places, her past and her present. When she left, she was a different person. Instead of avoiding people, she went straight into town to tell her neighbors about this man who knew everything about her—just as they knew everything about her—but who loved and accepted her nonetheless.

Jesus' actions remind me of Sir William Osler, one of the most esteemed physicians in modern medical history. The two-volume biography of his life depicts not only his genius as a physician, but also his qualities as a person. It is told that one day Osler entered a pediatric ward of a London hospital and noted with delight the children playing at one end of the room. Then his gaze was drawn to one small girl who sat off to one side, alone on her bed, a doll in her arms. She was clearly suffering from loneliness.

A question about her to the head nurse brought a response he suspected—the girl had been ostracized by the other children. Her mother was dead. Her father had paid but one visit, bringing the doll she now clutched tightly. Apart from that, no one had come to see her. The other children, concluding that she was unimportant, treated her with disdain.

Osler was at his best in moments like this, and he immediately walked over to the child's bed. "May I sit down?" he asked in a voice loud enough that the other children could hear. "I can't stay long on this visit, but I have wanted to see you so badly." Those describing the moment say that the girl's eyes became electric with joy.

For several minutes the physician conversed with her, in quieter tones. He asked about her doll's health and listened to the doll's heart with his stethoscope. Then, as he rose to leave, his voice lifted once more and said, "You won't forget our secret, will you? And mind you, don't tell anyone." As Osler left the room, the ignored child was now the center of attention.

I like to think something similar happened with Jesus and that woman at the well. Something electric took place. Her eyes began to sparkle again. Her self-esteem rose. She left that encounter with renewed hope because someone took an interest in her and loved and accepted who she was.

THE MINISTRY OF ACCEPTANCE

Following in Jesus' footsteps, the Apostle Paul invites us to participate in the ministry of acceptance. He wrote,

> Accept one another, then, just as Christ accepted you to
> bring praise to God. (Romans 15:7 NIV)

Other translations substitute the word "welcome" or "receive" for the word "accept." Using the very same word as in Romans 15:7, Paul also wrote:

> *Welcome* those who are weak in faith, but not for the purpose of quarreling over opinions. Some believe in eating anything, while the weak eat only vegetables. Those who eat must not despise those who abstain, and those who abstain must not pass judgment on those who eat; for God has *welcomed* them. Who are you to pass judgment on servants of one another? (Romans 14:1-4, *italics mine*)

To grasp the significance of this, we need to understand that the Church in ancient Rome divided itself into two camps, those who ate meat and those who did not. The meat-eaters lived by the counsel that Paul articulated in his Letter to the Corinthians: "Food will not bring us closer to God. We are not worse off if we do not eat, and no better if we do" (1 Corinthians 8:8). The meat-eaters, apparently the larger of the two groups, saw themselves as more mature in their faith because they were not tied to relics of a pagan or Jewish past. The vegetarians may well have been Jewish Christians who were concerned about the proper handling of slaughtered meat. If it was not kosher, they refused to eat it. Or the vegetarians could have been overly conscientious Christians who were concerned about meat offered to idols that may have later been sold to the local butcher. Regardless of the rationale, meat-eaters saw the "vegetarian" group as weak and avoided contact with them. The vegetarians and the meat-eaters despised one another. They had as much tolerance for one another as Rush Limbaugh has for a liberal Democrat.

The Apostle Paul suggested a new way of relating to one another: "Welcome those whom you consider to be weak in the faith. Welcome them because God has welcomed them and your actions will bring glory to God."

In other words, relationships are more important than doctrine. When we welcome and accept and receive those who are different from us into our circle of love, we are demonstrating God's transforming power working within us, and bringing honor and glory to God.

FOUR "WELCOMING" PRACTICES

Even when we have every good intention of being accepting, the question remains: How do we do it? How do we battle the tendency to judge rather than accept? How do we fight the desire to turn away rather than welcome? How do we become welcoming and receiving individuals? Here are four practices that can help:

• PRACTICE ONE: *Fight first impressions.*

A number of years ago, I was returning home from a Presbytery meeting in a very rural community in southwest Iowa. In the car on the way back, one of our elders, Shirley Nelson, told us about a dinner conversation she had with a retired pastor there. They had been discussing various topics when she asked him, "Do you get to Omaha very much?"

"No," he said. "It's an hour-and-a-half drive, and my wife and I are concerned about all the murders."

We chuckled at that comment. We had lived in the more populous locale of Omaha for years, and none of us remembered ever dodging bullets in the city. Some of us had even lived in Omaha our entire lives, and still no bullets. Later in the week, I began to feel sorry for that pastor because his first impression of Omaha was robbing him of some great times in "the big city." (And for all of you who have difficulty believing it, there are some wonderful things to do and see in Omaha, Nebraska!)

First impressions not only rob us of enjoying fun cities, they also rob of us getting to know some terrific people. I remember my first impression of a man named Tom Hayes—it was less than flattering. Tom was the principal of the middle school in Brookings, Oregon, where I served as a pastor. He appeared pompous, a real know-it-all. Our first conversation took place when he came into my office to chew me out for a decision I had made about firing the choir director. He walked out of my office saying, "You made a mistake firing that man."

Two weeks later, out of the blue, Tom invited me to play racquetball. I thought he wanted to use that as an excuse to bend my ear some more about rehiring the choir director, but he never brought the subject up. After knocking the ball around for an hour, I asked him, "Tom, is there anything special you wanted to talk about today in addition to playing racquetball?"

He replied, "No, I thought we got off on the wrong foot, and I just wanted to get to know you better."

That was the first of many racquetball games between us. We became close friends. In fact, he became a confidant.

That would never have happened if Tom had not taken the next step. My first impression almost kept me from a great friendship. Like Huck Finn said, "That's just the way with some people. They get down on a thing when they don't know nothin' about it."

This first practice asks you to fight through your first impressions. Start in your small group. As you get to know individual members, they will surprise you. The person who at first appears gruff may turn out to have a big heart. The quiet one may have more to say than you ever imagined. And "Mr. Rigid" may prove to be flexible at just the right moments.

● <u>PRACTICE TWO</u>: *Love, don't label.*

A man from Florida, Arthur M. Friedrichs, reflecting back on his New York school days wrote,

> For many years I rode the New York City subway to and from school. People are interesting to observe, and I found myself putting them into various categories. Not only did I decide how attractive or repulsive they were, how old they were, how rich or poor; I judged their character, deciding in my own mind whether they were good or bad people. Mentally I condemned some and praised others, disliking some and liking others.
>
> One day we students were given a test in class. We were given photos of one hundred people whom we had never seen. Below each photo was space for us to give our opinion as to each person's IQ, vocation, education, character, etc. I knew I would be good at this because of my experience in judging people I met on the subway. The results were fantastic. The entire class, including me, misjudged completely. We were wrong on most counts."[3]

I often find myself at the receiving end of the judging. When I fly, I get the inevitable question, "What do you do?" When I say, "I'm a Presbyterian pastor," they say, "Oh, I see," and they treat me differently. They attach a "clergy" label to me and put me in a box. Then they find something to read so they do not have to talk to the "religious guy" next to them.

I often wonder what other labels pop into their minds. Do they think I'm uptight? Maybe. No fun? Possibly. Liberal? Definitely. After all, you have to watch those Presbyterians!

Think of the labels we quickly hang on people:

"Oh, you're unemployed." Label: no marketable skills.

"So you are an accountant" Label: a real bore.

"He plays football." Label: no brains.

"I'm a Republican." Label: doesn't care for the poor.

"I'm a Democrat." Label: fiscally irresponsible.

"I'm from Paducah, Kentucky." Label: hick.

What labels have you already placed on the people in your group? Attention-seeker? Airhead? Loser? Prude? Nerd? This second practice asks you to remove preconceived labels. Your small group is a good place to start.

• PRACTICE THREE: *Let Scripture be the standard.*

A few years ago, Ross Robson retired from pastoral ministry. I knew Ross when he served the First Presbyterian Church in Omaha. In the mid-eighties Ross took a month and traveled through India, going from mission station to mission station. Knowing he would be in Calcutta, he decided, on a lark, to call Mother Teresa to see if he might be able to meet this great saint who chose a life of ministry to the hungry, the ill, the dying. Ross did not think it was possible, but he figured "nothing ventured, nothing gained." To his surprise, he was informed by the person answering the phone that he could indeed meet Mother Teresa on a Sunday afternoon at 2:00 P.M.

Ross spent a magnificent hour with her. In particular, he asked her, "How do you do it? How do you take the stench, the suffering?"

Mother Teresa responded by quoting Scripture: "As you have done it to the least of these, you have done it to me." Scripture was her standard.

According to Scripture, each person we meet is a valued and beloved child of God. This third practice asks you to work on seeing people through Christ's eyes: welcoming, accepting, and receiving each individual equally. The next time your group meets, see what a little "vision correction" does—for you and the group.

• PRACTICE FOUR: *Make mercy your message.*

Two experiences of my ministry stay with me. One happened in Brookings, Oregon. I was conducting worship, going through the morning announcements, when a young man in his mid-twenties with long hair and dirty clothes walked into the sanctuary with a young boy at his side and sat near the front. He obviously was different from others in the church that morning, and every eye in the sanctuary followed him to his seat, nervously glancing over at him during the service. No one said a word, but the mood of the congregation was anything but gracious. Finally, the man became so uncomfortable, he took his son's hand and, head bowed, left the sanctuary, before the service was over.

The other incident took place in my congregation in Omaha. I was greeting people at the back of the sanctuary after worship when I noticed a commotion in the narthex. I was not sure what was happening other than realizing that people were shifting away from the Welcome Center. Later I discovered the cause: a young man, similar to the one in Oregon—unkempt and a little odorous—was obviously not blending into this white-collar Presbyterian congregation. People had become so uncomfortable with him, they were literally fleeing the area. Our associate pastor, Jim Fiedler, came to the rescue. He walked over, befriended the man, offered him a cup of coffee, and introduced him to others in the congregation.

We never saw either man again. Maybe we would have if we had been more gracious and merciful, not so cold and quietly judgmental.

Something similar can happen in a small group. If someone does not "fit in" with the majority of group members, he or she can begin to feel like an outcast and will eventually leave. I am convinced that was the reason a woman named Meredith left our small group. We were white-collar people; Meredith was blue collar. Most of us drove newer automobiles; she drove a late model "junker." Most of us shopped at Dillards; she shopped at Wal-Mart. When she decided to leave the group, we did not put up a protest. She lived on the other side of town. She was not quite like us. We would not miss her all that much.

Someone once defined "grace" as not getting what we do deserve, and "mercy" as getting what we do not deserve. A small group is a good place to learn how to practice both.

C. S. Lewis, in *The Voyage of the Dawn Treader* story from the classic Narnia tales, gives us a vivid picture of loving and accepting people "warts and all." During the voyage Lucy undergoes a spell that allows her to see and hear what others are saying about her. Even though she is in Narnia, she can hear and see what others are saying about her in England. Under the spell she overhears one child say, "Not a bad little kid in her way. But I was getting pretty tired of her by the end of the term."

Lucy's response was fierce and immediate. Lucy did not want anything more to do with that girl. For Lucy, the friendship was over. She said, "Well you jolly well won't have the chance any other term. Two-faced little beast!"

What Lucy could not see, however, was that this girl really liked her. It was just that the girl was in the presence of older girls who were criticizing Lucy, so she was afraid to speak on behalf of her friend.

Aslan, the Christ figure in the story, does a great thing: He helps Lucy to see her friends as they really are, and to accept them in their weaknesses. He also helps her to see that her friends really do love her despite her weaknesses and frailties.[4]

Someone once said, "Jesus loves you, and I'm working on it!" This is the work of the fourth practice: to mirror Jesus' accepting, welcoming, and receiving presence on earth—starting with the people in your small group!

GROUP DISCUSSION AND SHARING

1. **Icebreaker** *(20-30 minutes)*
   - A time in my life when I felt out of place and unwelcome was . . .
   - A time when someone went out of his or her way to make me feel welcome was . . .

2. **Discussion** *(15-30 minutes)*
   - Name two things that stood out to you in this chapter.
   - What's the "up side" of being in an accepting and welcoming community? What is the "down side" or danger of being in such a community?

3. **Life Sharing** *(20-30 minutes)*
   - Where are you feeling out of place and unwelcome today? How are you feeling in this group? Are you feeling included or excluded, part of the gang or on the fringe?
   - Who in your circle of family, friends, or work associates especially needs to hear a word of acceptance rather than judgment or condemnation from you?

4. **Prayer** *(5 minutes)*
   Pray for the person on your left by completing this sentence:
   - "God, I thank you for *[PERSON'S NAME]* and hope that he/she will feel your presence this week."

CHAPTER FOUR

SERVE ONE ANOTHER

You . . . were called to be free.
But do not use your freedom
to indulge the sinful nature;
rather serve one another in love.
Galatians 5:13 NIV

For you were called to freedom, brothers and sisters;
only do not use your freedom
as an opportunity for self-indulgence,
but through love become slaves to one another.
Galatians 5:13 NRSV

* Bruce Hedgepeth loves to organize short-term mission trips. Each summer he takes a group of twenty people with him to Mexico's Yucatan Peninsula to serve and to learn from the Mayan people. Over the years Bruce and his short-term mission teams have built a sanctuary, a kitchen, and classrooms for a poor rural congregation in Samahil. He intends to return to the Yucatan for years to come.

* Irene Martin's heart beats for the down-and-out. On the twenty-fifth of each month, she coordinates meals for "Fresh Start." Based in Orlando, Florida, "Fresh Start" gives men and women a second chance, providing shelter, meals, and job training for homeless individuals who want to move off street and back into the work force. Irene comes to her church, collects the food members have donated, and takes three or four volunteers with her to serve dinner to

twenty to thirty men and women who work during the day and return to the shelter each night.

- Glenda Morgan gives one day a week to her church. Each Monday she comes to the church office to answer phones, take messages, and serve as a receptionist for the church staff. She has been doing this volunteer work for three years.

- Don Collins spends most Saturday mornings working on a local Habitat for Humanity house. During the week he calls volunteers, organizes the Saturday work crew and, then, on Saturdays supervises the crew he has recruited. A contractor by trade, he receives no financial remuneration for his labors. He just enjoys using his talents for the good of others.

- Albert Schweitzer, who spent fifty years of his life serving humanity in the oppressive heat of the African jungle, providing medical aid to those most desperately in need, said, "I don't know what your destiny will be, but one thing I do know; the only ones among you who will be happy are those who have sought and found how to serve."[1]

- Robert Schuller preaches, "Ego fulfillment comes through service, not status."[2]

- One of the early pioneers of the American West, Bryant S. Hinckley, said, "Service is the virtue that distinguished the great of all times and which they will be remembered by. It places a mark of nobility upon its disciples. It is the dividing line which separates the two great groups of the world—those who help and those who hinder, those who lift and those who lean, those who contribute and those who only consume. How much better it is to give than to receive. Service in any form is comely and beautiful. To give encouragement, to impart sympathy, to show interest, to banish fear, to build self-confidence and awaken hope in the hearts of others, in short—to love them and to show it—is to render the most precious service."[3]

THE SERVANT'S MODEL

Jesus went about the countryside putting the "theory" of service into action, stating, "For the Son of Man came not to be served but to serve" (Mark 10:45). Even the night of his arrest, he was still putting those words into action. Jesus and his disciples had gathered in the Upper Room for the most sacred of Jewish feasts, the Passover meal, and just as they were about to bite into their salads, Jesus realized something was wrong. He realized no one had taken time to wash their feet when they entered the room.

In New Testament times, every walk in the streets soiled sandaled feet. During the dry season, sandaled feet would get dusty. During wet weather, they would become caked with mud. As a result, just inside the doorway of most homes sat a water basin with a towel. A servant stationed at the door would greet people and wash their feet as they entered the house.

On the night of Jesus' arrest, however, no one had assumed this menial task. Maybe they had gotten caught up in their celebrity status. After all, Jesus and the disciples were the talk of the town. They had entered the city to shouts of "Hosanna" and "Blessed is he who comes in the name of the Lord." To be associated with Jesus was parallel to getting the best table at restaurants, court-side seats at basketball games, and invitations to the best parties. Celebrities do not wash feet. Celebrities bask in the light of acclaim.

Or maybe they did not want to hurt Jesus' feelings by pointing out the omission. After all, Jesus had arranged for the room and the meal. If he had forgotten to station a servant at the door to wash feet, well, it was just a small oversight. Let's not ruin a great evening by complaining about no one to wash our feet. We'll just eat with dirty feet tonight. It's no big deal.

Or maybe they expected one of the "lesser" disciples to do it. Read through the list of the Apostles and you will notice a "pecking order." The Gospel writers divided the disciples into three groups. The first group contained Peter, James, John, and Andrew. Among the Twelve, they were the most influential. The middle group contained Philip, Bartholomew, Matthew, and Thomas. These were noteworthy individuals but a notch below the first group in stature. Bringing up the rear were James son of Alphaeus, Thaddeus, Simon the Canaean, and Judas Iscariot. Given his betrayal of Jesus, we know why the Gospel writers listed Judas last.

So maybe the disciples were waiting for James the Lesser or Thaddeus or Simon the Canaean to wash their feet. Maybe they were even motioning one of them to get up from the table to wash their feet. Given the fact that the Gospel writer Luke tells us that the disciples engaged in a dispute that night as to who was the greatest suggests such a scenario was well within the realm of possibility (Luke 22:24-30)!

Whatever the reason, Jesus got up from the table, poured water into a basin, and began to wash the disciples' feet. His actions shocked Peter, the number-one disciple. His response to Jesus was, "You will never wash my feet." He obviously felt this menial task was below Jesus, that a servant did this type of work, not a man of Jesus' status.

Jesus' behavior reminds me of another man who was overdressed for his assignment and out of character for his immediate job. He was whistling while he toiled, smiling and greeting others as they entered the men's room. This jovial man was removing cigarette butts from the bathroom urinals, utilizing small scissors to retrieve the soggy and offensive stubs.

"That's not an envious job you're doing," said one of the restroom patrons.

"No, sir! No, sir! It's not! But it must be done. Looks bad when customers come into the bathroom. Makes people think we don't care or that we are not clean. So, I clean them up everyday."

"Do men throw their cigarette butts in the urinal very often?" the patron inquired.

"Often????!!!! Every morning I pick up six, seven, sometimes sixteen cigarettes just out of one urinal!"

"Why do people throw them in there?" he asked.

"Lazy, just lazy. Or they don't care. Maybe they never were raised any better. Maybe they have never grown up. Perhaps they do it out of meanness," he whispered determinedly under his breath. "And maybe they never had to clean up after themselves."

The patron, while washing his hands, asked, "You been working here long?"

The answer startled the patron. "I don't work here," said the man. "I come here almost every day over the noon hour and eat. I have an office across the street."

"YOU WHAT??? You don't work here, and you clean up the bathroom? Why do you do it?"

"Because of the next man who comes in here and uses this place. I want him to notice the area is clean and that someone cares."

"Even if he throws a cigarette butt into your freshly cleaned urinal?" asked the patron. He was getting edgy.

"Doesn't matter," said the man. "What counts is that this facility is clean for an hour, maybe two. And if the man comes in here and notices this bathroom is clean and he enjoys himself, just maybe he will comprehend the cleanness and leave the bathroom a better place when he walks out of here."

The patron dried his hands, and all of a sudden found himself wiping up the extra water around the sink and cleaning the water droplets from the mirror. While throwing the paper towel in the trash, he noticed a piece of wet, paper towel on the floor. He picked it up, placed it in the trash can, and left the restroom. A few minutes later, as he was eating his lunch, he noticed the "urinal cleaner" walking and whistling his way out of the building, straightening his tie, and sauntering across the street to his office.

What Jesus did was just as shocking to Peter. How could Jesus stoop so low as to wash his feet? How could the eternal Son of God get on his knees to wash the feet of those who should have been washing *his* feet? He did it to model a behavior and drive home a point. The Gospel writer John tells us,

> After he had washed their feet, had put on his robe, and had returned to the table, he said to them, "Do you know what I have done to you? You call me Teacher and Lord—and you are right for that is what I am. So, if I, your Lord and Teacher, have washed your feet, you also ought to wash one another's feet. For I have set you an example, that you also should do as I have done to you. (John 13:12-15)

What does this mean for us? In part, it means we are called to be servants. Jesus wants us to have the very thing that set him apart from the people of his day: a servant's heart.

In the late seventies James B. Irwin, the former astronaut, addressed the National Religious Broadcasters convention in Washington, D.C. He spoke of the thrill of leaving the earth's atmosphere. He spoke of the strangeness of seeing the earth shrink in size as he traveled closer to the moon. He spoke of the privilege of being part of a crew who had made a successful moonwalk. He also spoke of watching the earth "rise" one morning on his way back to the planet and thinking he would probably be a celebrity when he returned home. He knew talk show hosts would want him to be a guest. He knew reporters would seek interviews. But perhaps the most powerful thing he told those at the convention was this humble statement: "As I was returning to earth, I realized that I was a servant—not a celebrity. So I am here as God's servant on planet Earth to share what I have experienced that others might know the glory of God."[4]

James Irwin was right on the mark. In God's family there is to be but one great body of people: all servants, no celebrities.

THE SERVANT'S MINDSET

The Apostle Paul writes,

> Have the same mind in you that was in Christ Jesus, who though he was in the form of God, did not regard equality with God as something to be exploited, but emptied himself, taking the form of a slave, being born in human likeness. (Philippians 2:5-7)

Most of us are familiar with the term "upward mobility." The American Dream espouses it. The economy depends on it. The "Jeffersons" lived it—their television sitcom opened with the words, "We're moving on up to the East Side." Jesus, however, practiced *downward* mobility. He emptied himself, taking the form of a "slave" or a "servant." He climbed down the ladder to us, and we are to have the same mindset.

In 1953 Sir Edmund Hillary climbed to the summit of Mount Everest, the first man ever to do so. Hillary got all the press, but critical to his ascent was one of Sir Edmund's climbing companions, Tenzig Norgay.

No one ever mentions Norgay's name, yet on the way back down the mountain, Hillary fell and would have been killed if Tenzig Norgay had not pulled him back up by cable and saved his life. Hillary lived to tell a great story due to the help of an unknown man. When someone asked Norgay why he did not brag about it, he replied, "We mountain climbers help each other."[5]

This is what servant-heart people do. They help one another.

I think back to the time in our small group when Dara arrived an hour late. We were just ready to take our break, but it was obvious she was distressed. After wrapping up business matters in Tampa, she had driven back to Orlando—a two-hour drive—to be with our group. When she arrived, we could tell she had been crying.

The leader proceeded to ask the group a few more general questions concerning the study, and then said, "Dara, before we break, we would sure like to hear about you and your day."

Dara talked for the next twenty-five minutes. Emotions poured out of her—anger, tears, frustration, embarrassment. She was devastated. Earlier in the afternoon she had been told that she was no longer being considered for the educational trainer position for which she had interviewed. As I sat there, I was aware that listening to Dara was the most important thing we could be doing. As a group we were there to help Dara. That is what servants do for one another.

I am reminded of the story told of a woman in tattered clothes, standing on a big city street corner with her sad-looking little boy, begging for food or money to buy food. It so happened that among the passersby was a wealthy man who looked at them but did not offer any help. When he arrived at his palatial home and looked at his dinner table laden with the finest foods, he began to think about the poor little waif and his distressed mother. The more he thought about the situation, the angrier he became at God. Then he clenched his fist and shook it in what he thought to be God's direction. He cried out, "How can you allow such misery? Why don't you do something to help those unfortunate people?"

Then, somewhere deep within himself came God's answer: "I did. I created you."

People with servant hearts know that. They know they are there to aid others.

THE SERVANT'S PERIL

Of course, given their propensity to help others, people with servant hearts need to guard against burnout. They need to guard against losing themselves in others. They need to set limits. They need to realize they do not have to meet every need and every cry for help. If they do not realize this, their emotional reserves will quickly become depleted. They will find their zest for life gone, and their daily lives will consist of the "toos"—too many pressures, too many needs, too many things to get done, too few accomplishments, and too few rewards.

Nazarene pastor David McKellips says God's servants need to guard against "getting splashed"[6] Have you ever been splashed? I am not talking about having water splashed on you. I am talking about what often occurred in the Chicago Bears locker room back in the early nineties.

The defensive backs and the defensive lineman played a little game, and if you lost, you got splashed. Here is how it worked. Defensive backs and defensive linemen would verbally assault one another. Then the linemen would try to encircle one of the defensive backs. On most occasions, the quicker defensive backs were able to strike with a verbal assault and quickly escape. But if captured, they paid a great price.

Defensive back David Tate, who weighed 180 pounds, was splashed. He was dropped to the ground, and the 325-pound William "The Refrigerator" Perry collapsed on top of him. Then the 270-pound Richard Dent jumped on him, followed by the 275-pound Dan Hampton and the 270-pound Steve McMichael. In other words, if you were a defensive back for the Chicago Bears back in 1990 and you got splashed, 1,140 pounds of pain came down on top of you.

David Tate said of his "splashing" experience, "It hurts. I don't think they know how heavy they are. Once you've gotten 'splashed,' you avoid it at all costs, even if it means backing down."

People with servant hearts often get splashed—not by defensive linemen but by schedule overload and commitment overload and expectation overload and emotional overload and people overload and problem overload. Dr. Richard Swenson claims many servants are being "splashed" regularly:

> The spontaneous tendency of our culture is to inexorably add detail to our lives: one more option, one more problem, one more commitment, one more expectation, one more purchase, one more debt, one more decision. We must now deal with more "things per person" than at any other time in history. Yet one can comfortably handle only so many details in his or her life. . . . Overloading occurs whenever the requirements upon us exceed that which we are able to bear. For example, camels are able to carry great loads. If, however, a mere straw is placed on a camel maximally loaded down, its back will be broken. The back is not broken by the proverbial straw, it's broken by overload.[7]

Someone once said, "If you burn the candle at both ends, you are not as bright as you think you are." Wise servants learn when to say, "Yes" and when to say, "No." Wise servants learn how to take care of themselves. Wise servants practice three "C's": concentration, clarification, and "clear"ifcation.

THE SERVANT'S PRACTICE

First, wise servants CONCENTRATE on God. They regularly seek God's face. I think of the man who came across three boys playing in the snow. He came up to them and asked, "Would you like to try a race and the winner win a prize?"

They boys said, "Yes," and the man told them the race would be different. He said, "I will go to the other side of the field, and when I give you the signal, you start to run. The one whose footsteps are straightest in the snow will be the winner."

So the race started, and the first boy watched his feet to make sure he was running as straight as possible. The second lad did the same. He watched his feet. The third boy, however, did something different. He ran with his eyes steadfastly fixed on the man at the other side of the field, and he won! Because he had kept his eyes on the goal ahead of him, his footsteps were straight in the snow.

Do you know why animal trainers carry a stool or a chair when they get into a cage of lions? They have a whip, of course, and a pistol at their sides, but have you ever wondered about the stool? Well, to the lion tamer the stool is the most important piece of equipment. When the lion tamer holds the back of the stool and thrusts the stool's legs at the lion, the lion focuses on all four legs at once. And, in the attempt to focus on all four, a kind of paralysis overwhelms the animal; it becomes weak and disabled because its attention is fragmented.

A singular focus is the essence of Jesus' command, "Seek ye first the Kingdom of God": concentrate on that one thing, and all other things will fall into place in our lives.

Second, wise servants CLARIFY. When Jesus summarized the law in two commandments, his instructions were clear. Commandment one: Love God with all your heart, soul, strength, and mind. Commandment two: Love your neighbor as you love yourself.

These two commandments clarify where we are to spend our time. Our first priority is to spend time growing in our faith, drawing closer to God. Then we are to spend time taking care of ourselves. If we do not take care of ourselves by getting enough sleep and exercise and by eating properly, we will not have the strength to serve others over the long haul. Only then can we love our neighbors. Wise servants keep these priorities in their basic relationships: God, self, others (family, church, work, world).

I think of Billy Graham and how his concentrated times with God have led to great clarity in his life. A number of years ago, Dr. Graham was asked to be the commencement speaker at Seattle Pacific University, a Christian school. David McKenna, who extended the invitation, pulled out all the stops. McKenna told Dr. Graham that commencement was a grand occasion for the University, held in the exquisite Seattle Opera House. Dr. Graham listened patiently to the offer, mused a moment, and then answered, "David, I'm flattered by your invitation, but I must say, 'No.' You see, God has called me to be an evangelist. I would find it a joy to be with you, knowing that I would be among Christian friends, but if I say 'Yes,' I would have to turn down an invitation to preach where other men and women have not preached."[8]

Finally, wise servants "CLEAR"IFY. By that, I mean they clear the clutter from their lives so they can serve most effectively.

I think of the events from the sixth chapter of Acts. The Apostles were in hot water. They were being criticized for dropping the ball. The non-Hebrew widows in Jerusalem were complaining about being overlooked in the daily food distribution. The twelve called together the whole community and said, "It is not right that we should neglect the word of God in order to wait on tables. Therefore, friends, select from among yourselves seven men of good standing, full of the Holy Spirit and of wisdom, whom we may appoint to this task, while we, for our part, will devote ourselves to prayer and to serving the word" (Acts 6:2-4).

Do you see what the Apostles did? They cleared some "service" expectations from their lives. Through previous concentrated times with God, they had clarified their purpose. They were to pray and preach the word, and not be the widows' primary caregivers. Taking care of the widows was not their designated responsibility. Though the needs were genuine, God did not call the Apostles to meet them personally.

THE SERVANT'S REWARD

Serving others, though costly in terms of time and energy, pays great dividends. Ask Dr. Ken Bailey, a Presbytery missionary scholar. He taught at a seminary in Jerusalem and became friends of the priest of a nearby Greek Catholic Church. One day, a bomb was detonated outside the beautiful doors of the church. The doors were blown inward, destroying the altar. Windows were destroyed, and a third of the pews were ruined. The priest was devastated.

Dr. Bailey, seeing his friend in such pain, immediately went to work. He persuaded leaders of the seminary to close down classes for a day so that students might join him in helping the priest. Dr. Bailey and the students started with something very practical. They boarded up the building so that it could not be looted. The next day, with the building safe from looters, Dr. Bailey went to visit the priest at the rectory. The maid confided to him that the priest did not cry at the bomb's destruction. She added, "However, he did cry when you and your friends helped clean up the mess it made."

Some of the rewards, like the tears of the Greek Catholic priest, we receive here on earth. Another reward awaits us in heaven—God's applause.

I am reminded of the missionary couple returning to the States after years of overseas service. As fortune would have it, they were sailing on the same ship on which President Teddy Roosevelt was returning. The President had just completed another of his big-game expeditions.

The missionary couple watched as people clamored to see the President and to welcome him home, but there was no such welcome for them. Despondent, the husband said to his wife, "Something is wrong. Why should we have given our lives in faithful service for God in Africa all these many years and have no one care a thing about us? Here this man comes back from a hunting trip, and everybody makes much over him, but nobody gives two hoots about us."

That night the man grew angrier and said to his wife, "I can't take this. God is not treating us fairly!"

She said, "Tell God about it in prayer," and he did. He went into the bedroom to pray, and a short time later he came out of the bedroom with his spirit obviously lifted.

"Dear, what happened?" she inquired.

He replied, "The Lord settled it with me. I told him how bitter I was that the President should receive this tremendous homecoming when no one met us as we returned home. And when I finished, it seemed as though the Lord put his hand on my shoulder and simply said, 'But you are not home yet!' "

When this missionary does return "home," God's welcoming words await him: "Well done, good and faithful servant."

SERVICE IN SMALL GROUPS

One of the more rewarding experiences a group can have is serving others. Working side-by-side as a group brings people together in a most significant way. Small groups in our congregation have volunteered to work together on Habitat Houses, to serve meals at local shelters, to greet visitors on Sunday mornings, and to paint classrooms. After such efforts, I hear people make such comments as, "Why don't we do this more often?" or "It felt good to make a difference."

Group members can also have fun serving each other. I will long remember the time my wife, Trudy, and I volunteered to take care of Bob and Vicki Gramann's infant daughter, Alicia. The Gramanns were in our small group, and they had to attend a conference for the weekend. We asked if we might watch their daughter. When they dropped Alicia off on their way out of town, Vicki handed us a pacifier and a tub of whipped honey, saying, "If Alicia cries, dip the pacifier in the honey. That calms her down." Well, cry she did. In fact, when Bob and Vicki returned, the tub was almost empty! Vicki took one look at the almost-empty tub and our bleary eyes, and exclaimed, "We're sorry."

We were not. We enjoyed our time with Alicia, and we loved doing something special for our friends. If we had not been willing to babysit, we would have missed out on that fond memory.

A number of other people come to mind: Don Plane likes to cook for his small group. Once a quarter he invites his group to a picnic at a park. He buys all the food and grills in the great outdoors. You should see the smile on his face as group members "dig in" to what he has lovingly prepared. Madge Sutcliffe serves her group by volunteering to order and pick up the books for her small group's new study. Craig Fuhrman serves his group by calling all the members when there is a change in meeting places.

How might your small group be of service to your community, your church, and to each other? Do not miss the joy of going the extra mile for someone else.

GROUP DISCUSSION AND SHARING

1. **Icebreaker** *(10-15 minutes)*
    - When recently did someone "go the extra mile" for you or when recently did you "go the extra mile" for them?

2. **Discussion** *(20-30 minutes)*
    - What does it mean to you to have a servant's heart?
    - What do you see as the benefits of serving others? What rewards do you think a servant receives?
    - What are some obstacles to being a good and faithful servant?
    - What particularly struck you—positively or negatively—in this chapter?

3. **Life Sharing** *(25-35 minutes)*
    - Where are you finding it hard to be a servant? Where is it easy?
    - How might your group team together in service?
    - How can the group be praying for you?

4. **Prayer** *(5-10 minutes)*
    Divide the time between thanksgiving and requests.
    - Begin with the leader saying, "God, we thank you for . . ." and have members share a word or phrase that comes to mind.
    - Then have the leader say, "God we bring our concerns before you. Please be with . . ." and have members respond with a word or phrase, such as, "Frank's job interview," "Sarah's daughter," "Betsy's doctor appointment."

CHAPTER FIVE

BE KIND TO ONE ANOTHER

Put away from you all bitterness and wrath and anger
and wrangling and slander, together with all malice,
and be kind to one another . . .
Ephesians 4:31-32

By contrast, the fruit of the Spirit is love, joy, peace, patience,
kindness, generosity, faithfulness,
gentleness, and self-control.
Galatians 5:22

We do not remember her name—only her kindness to us. Trudy and I had been married five days. We were driving Trudy's car from Los Angeles to Boise, Idaho, where I would be working as Program Director for the YMCA. Unfortunately, Trudy's car gave us fits every mile of the way. Something was wrong with the engine, and it burned two quarts of oil every hundred miles of the trip. Finally, one late afternoon, the car broke down in a desolate section of eastern Oregon about eighty miles from Boise. As a result, we ended up hitchhiking on our honeymoon!

Out of nowhere, a woman stopped. She asked what was wrong. We told her our sad story, and she took us to the nearest service station, which proved to be fifteen miles down the highway. Instead of dropping us off and driving away, however, she said, "Let's see what they tell you before I go on."

When she heard that they would not be able to fix our car for a couple of days, she asked us, "I'm sorry, I have forgotten. Where did you say you are going?" After we said, "Boise," she said, "Hop in the car. I'll take you there." And she did, all the way to our doorstep.

A week later I drove back to the service station and picked up the car.

We don't remember her name, but twenty-eight years later we still remember her kindness to us.

Our son Josh was touched by someone with a similar spirit. Though her act of kindness was not as sacrificial, it still made a huge impression on our son. Taking the tollway from the airport, Josh went to pay his fifty-cent toll, only to have the attendant say, "It's already paid for. The woman in the car ahead of you treated you." Josh was so impressed by her kindness that, at the next toll booth, he paid for himself and the person behind him! Who knows what the person behind him did. All I know, Josh was all smiles when he arrived home. He had a fantastic trip from the airport all because a woman paid for his toll.

Of course, one has to be careful with these acts of kindness. I think of the patrol officer who arrived at the scene of an accident to find a woman lying unconscious a few feet from an automobile. A small crowd had gathered, and a man was trying feverishly to revive the woman.

"Who was driving the car?" the officer asked.

"I was," answered the man who was helping the woman.

"How did you hit her?" the officer asked.

"Oh, I didn't hit her," the man said. "As I approached the intersection, I saw that she was trying to cross the street. So I stopped for her and she fainted."

We may not faint dead away when a stranger does something nice for us, but in a cutthroat, dog-eat-dog world, acts of kindness surprise us. They catch us off guard. We do not expect them, but we sure enjoy being on the receiving end of them—and it is just as fun to be an initiator of a kindness.

A FRUIT OF THE SPIRIT

The Apostle Paul encourages us to have such fun. He encourages us to be kind to one another. In fact, he lists kindness as a mark of Christian maturity and identifies it as one of the fruits of the Spirit: love, joy, peace, patience, *kindness*, goodness, faithfulness, gentleness and self-control (Galatians 5:22-23).

The Greek word for the fruit of kindness is *chrestotes*. Distinctive to Christianity, this Greek word was scarcely used outside of Christian literature, and unlike the first four fruits—love, joy, peace, patience—*chrestotes* is a distinctly external rather than internal quality.

Maybe you recall the old advertising campaign for "Weebles." Weebles were small plastic characters with rounded bases that stood about three inches high. Inside the Weeble, at the base, was a weight. When you tried to knock the character down, the internal anchor would keep it steady, and it would pop right back up. The advertising slogan for this unique children's toy was, "Weebles wobble but they don't fall down."

The first four fruits of the Spirit—love, joy, peace, patience—are a lot like Weebles. They provide internal stability in the midst of external pressure and adversity. No matter how frustrating people can be, no matter how hectic life can become, no matter how sad the news, love, joy, peace, and patience pop us back up. They give us an internal anchor.

Kindness, on the other hand, is best described by the old "Ma Bell" commercial, "Reach out and touch someone." Kindness is a distinctly external virtue. When we speak of kindness, an internal experience will not suffice. We cannot hold kindness inside. We have to express it. We have to reach out and touch someone.

In fact, the Apostle Paul commands it of us. As Jesus commanded us to love one another (John 13:34), Paul commands us to be kind to one another. In his letter to the Ephesians, Paul writes, "Be kind to one another, tenderhearted, forgiving one another, as God in Christ has forgiven you" (Ephesians 4:32).

Several biblical examples spring to mind. One is the Old Testament story of Ruth. The tale begins with a man named Elimelech, who migrated with his wife, Naomi, and his two sons, Mahlon and Chlilion, to the country of Moab because of a famine in their home of Bethlehem. While in Moab, the boys married two Moabite women, Orpah and Ruth. Then all three men died, leaving Naomi and her two daughters-in-law to fend for themselves. Shortly thereafter, Naomi heard that the famine in Bethlehem had ended, and she decided to return home. She encouraged Orpah and Ruth to remain in Moab with their families. Orpah decided to stay, but Ruth had different ideas. She said to her mother-in-law, "Do not press me to leave you or turn back from following you! Where you go, I will go; Where you lodge, I will lodge; your people shall be my people and your God my God" (Ruth 1:16).

In Bethlehem, Ruth continued to perform more and more acts of kindness, which resulted in her catching the eye of a man named Boaz. Ruth and Boaz eventually married, and they had a son named Obed. If proof were ever needed of the importance of one small act of kindness, here it is: their son, Obed, was the father of Jesse, who was the father of King David, from whom we can trace Jesus' lineage.

Another biblical example of kindness is the New Testament story of the Good Samaritan (Luke 10). A lawyer, testing Jesus, asked what he had to do to inherit eternal life. Jesus, however, turned the question back on the lawyer and asked what *he* thought the Scriptures said. The lawyer responded that to inherit eternal life, he had to love God and neighbor. Jesus told him he was right, but the lawyer continued to press, asking Jesus to define what the Scriptures meant by the term "neighbor." In response Jesus told this story:

> A man traveling the dangerous road from Jerusalem to Jericho was beaten and robbed and left for dead. A priest, a member of the highest echelon of temple authorities, was the first to encounter him. The priest passed him by, torn by a dilemma: If the man were dead and the priest touched him, then the priest would be defiled and unable to perform his Temple duties for seven days. If he helped the man, the priest would be unable to help hundreds of people later in the week.
>
> Later, a Levite saw the same man lying on the side of the road, but concerned it might be a trap, he, too, walked on by the injured man. He had heard the stories of bandits using decoys and was not about to be taken in. He would not take the risk of helping someone who may or may not be in need.
>
> And then, along came the Samaritan. His love for others spilled over into an amazing act of kindness. He cleaned the injured man's wounds and saw to it that the man was cared for. By this act of kindness the Samaritan communicated that the man was more important to him than the demands of his work or the potential danger that he faced in tending to him.

When Jesus asked the lawyer which man was a neighbor to the one who was robbed, the lawyer immediately recognized that it was the one who had demonstrated kindness. Jesus response was, "Go and do likewise."

I find it interesting that the heroes in both stories were "foreigners"—a Moabite woman and Samaritan man. Could it be that the biblical writers had a point to make about the people of God? Could it be that the biblical writers did not see much kindness being practiced among people of faith? Were the people of God so insensitive to one another that the biblical writers had to look outside the community of faith for inspirational examples of "kindness"? Or was it just a coincidence that both stories have heroes from outside Israel?

We cannot say for sure. I do know, however, that some of the meanest people I know can quote the Bible forward and backward. They are familiar with biblical facts but have never translated the gospel into their lives. They know Christ came to bring good news, but they do not pass along that good news to others. Paul must have known similar people in First Church Ephesus. As a result he commanded them, and he commanded us, "Be kind to one another."

How do we do that? Let me suggest three practices.

THREE "KINDNESS" PRACTICES

● <u>PRACTICE ONE</u>: *Recognize that all people have wounds.*

The first step in developing the fruit of kindness is to realize that all people have hurts—including the people in your small group.

Warren Magnuson, at one time an executive officer of the Baptist General Conference, certainly operated under that assumption. After preaching the Sunday sermon, Magnuson greeted people at the door. A woman on her way out of the sanctuary asked if she might see him a moment. So after he finished greeting the worshippers, he met with her in his office. Realizing her concerns needed more attention, he made an appointment for her to see him later in the week. Magnuson then went to join his wife. When he arrived at the car his wife said, "Warren, we are late for a luncheon engagement. We have to hurry."

"I know," he countered, "but the lady had to see me about a problem."

That afternoon the Magnusons enjoyed a lovely luncheon with gracious hosts. As they were leaving, however, one of the luncheon guests walked Magnuson to the car and told him of some difficulties he was having with his teenage son. He wanted to visit further, and Magnuson assured him that a time could be arranged that week. As Magnuson looked over the man's shoulder in the direction of the car, he noticed his wife pointing to her watch. He told the man to call the office tomorrow, excused himself, and joined his wife. As they drove off she reminded him, "We'll be late for the dedication service at the new church. We have to hurry."

"I know we're late," Magnuson replied, "but the man had a problem with his son and we had to talk."

After the dedication service came a reception with refreshments. Magnuson sat down with a cup of coffee next to a man he did not know. They introduced themselves and Magnuson asked, "Where are you from?"

"Michigan," the man replied.

"Do you have a family?"

The man's face dropped, and he began sharing how he and his wife were separated. He asked for counsel and they began sharing. When there was a break in the conversation, Magnuson looked up and saw his wife giving him another sign to hurry. He made an appointment with the man from Michigan, dismissed himself, and joined his rather exasperated wife.

"Warren," she said, "we have to hurry or we will be late for the evening service."

Magnuson replied, "I know, Margaret, but this man had some problems we needed to discuss."

Shaking her head she said, "Warren, how come you always sit next to people with problems?"

His reply was quick and simple. "Dear, whenever you sit next to people, you sit next to a problem."

So true. Wherever we are, whether a basketball game or PTA meeting, a coffee shop or a worship service—or a small group—we are sitting next to a problem. Just because everything on the outside appears calm does not mean it is. The person sitting next to us may be suffering from loneliness, physical pain, depression, low self-esteem, frustration over a job, or a broken relationship. We may not know their need, but we can be assured of a broken place in their lives.

The prophet Isaiah described the coming servant of Israel, the Christ, as one who would be sensitive to the people around him:

> Here is my servant, whom I behold,
> my chosen in whom my soul delights;
> I have put my spirit upon him;
> he will bring forth justice to the nations.
> He will not cry or lift up his voice,
> or make it heard in the street;
> a bruised reed he will not break,
> and a dimly burning wick he will not quench . . .
> (Isaiah 42:1-3)

Kind people know others are bruised and need special care. Kind people treat each other with tender compassion and understanding.

● <u>PRACTICE TWO</u>: *Fracture your schedule for others.*

Life's hurts do not come at the most convenient times. One simple way to practice kindness is to make extra time for people.

How do you usually handle interruptions? Do you view them as God's calling card or as a derailment? I suspect we all are a little like Mark Twain, who wrote the following holiday message in the *New York World:*

> It is my heart-warm and world-embracing Christmas hope and aspiration that all of us—the high, the low, the rich, the poor, the admired, the despised, the loved, the hated, the civilized, the savage—may eventually be gathered together in a heaven of everlasting bliss—except the inventor of the telephone.[1]

One wonders what Twain would think today in today's world of pagers, cell phones, and faxes! I certainly understand his sentiments. Each day I hope to make it through with a minimum of interruptions. I thrive on structure. I go through a similar routine most every morning: I arrive at office, turn on the computer, fill my coffee cup with hot water (I drink hot water not coffee or tea . . . I know, it's strange), take fifteen or twenty minutes for prayer, and then get to work. One might call it "clergy cocooning," but I like to protect my schedule. I thrive on quiet days of study and sermon writing. I am an extremely productive person, and I get a lot accomplished protecting my schedule. People, however, have a way of dropping in without appointments. They say things like, "Are you busy? Do you have a moment?" Telephones ring when I am just at a crucial point in sermon preparation and I lose my train of thought.

God is teaching me to be more flexible and to see interruptions as a divine calling card. God is teaching me to have a freedom and flexibility in my schedule that allows me to flow into situations where people are in need. Do not get me wrong. I am not saying to be kind means to throw your appointment book out the window, but to be kind God does call us, at times, to set aside our schedule in order to lend a listening ear, a warm hug, or a kind word.

I think of the mother and daughter who were on their way to have brunch with friends after worship. Already late, they rushed into the restaurant, but instead of joining their friends, the mother walked over to a woman eating alone, who looked extremely unhappy. The mother said to the woman, "Excuse me, but you remind me so much of my mother. Would you mind if I gave you a hug?"

The older woman beamed and gratefully accepted the hug. It obviously meant a lot to her.

"That was really sweet, Mom," the daughter said as they walked to find their friends, "but I didn't think she looked at all like Grandma."

"Nor did I," said the mother cheerfully.

Kind people have a knack for taking a minute here and there to fracture their schedules for others.

● PRACTICE THREE: *Don't just reach, touch.*

Perhaps one of the most visible practices of kindness is when we make a special effort to reach out and touch someone with a *tangible* act of kindness. A number of people in my life come to mind. I think of Kay Bahl, who took the time to write me this thank you note:

> Dear Dick,
>   Thank you for the beautiful way that you pre-sented the Bibles to the third graders. Your introduc-tion was special, and as you know, children think it's exciting to receive their very own Bible from the church.
>   Also, this sermon series has been most helpful to me. I've been tacking my notes to the refrigerator door. Incidentally, my husband's wife has as much trouble with patience as your wife's husband!
> Your friend in Christ,
Kay Bahl

I cannot express how much that little note of kindness meant to me.

I also think of some young couples in a small group. They had been meeting together for some time and had become close to one an-other. They shared their lives with each other, prayed for one another, and studied the Bible together. One of the couples in the group be-came pregnant with their second child. When the time came for the child to be born, everything went as planned—at first. Then the doctors told the parents their newborn was not doing well. The child had picked up an infection during birth. They were not sure whether the baby would live, and the parents asked the members of their small group to pray for their baby. That week, during the small group's regular meeting time, instead of gathering for Bible study and prayer time as usual, the other couples cleaned the house, washed and ironed clothes, and did the yard work for the couple who were spending all of their time at the hospital. The sick infant got better and the parents resumed a more normal pace of life, and the group developed a special bond with one another due to the tangible act of kindness.

Then there was the time two couples in the same small group traveled to Miami to see the Dolphins play a football game at the Orange Bowl. They parked their car some distance from the stadium on a dead-end street in a bad part of the city. The four had arrived early enough to grab a bite to eat at a fried chicken fast-food restaurant just around the corner from where they parked. While they ate at a table next to the window, a street person stood on the sidewalk watching them. At first they tried to ignore him. He was dirty and shabbily dressed. The man, however, continued to watch them eat. When they were finished, they left quickly out another door. When they got to the sidewalk, one of the husbands, Ivor Singer, asked the others to wait for him for a minute. Ivor disappeared back into the restaurant while the others waited nervously in a dangerous section of Miami. He rejoined the group and told them he just had to buy that man on the sidewalk a dinner.

But the story did not end there. As they walked to the Orange Bowl, the man from the sidewalk passed them with the box of chicken in his hands. "God bless you," he said to Ivor and turned down the dead-end street where the couples had parked their car. About halfway down the street, he stopped and set the chicken dinner down on the sidewalk. He then reached into a tall hedge and lifted out another man who had been hidden by the bushes. The man had no legs and only one arm. The dirty man from the sidewalk gently propped up the man with no legs. He opened the box of chicken and began to feed his friend.

Kindness—it may be a phone call asking someone how they are doing, a birthday card to a friend, a casserole for a neighbor who is sick. It is reaching out in a tangible way to care for someone—and it does wonders for the giver as well as the receiver.

Take the Japanese man who had just irrigated his rice field the previous day. It was very important at that time of the year to keep the field in standing water. The next day, however, when he went back to check on his field, all the water was gone. After looking around a bit, he discovered that his neighbor just down the hill had broken the dividing wall between their fields and drained the water to his own field.

This infuriated the man, so he went to consult with his pastor as to what he should do. The pastor advised the man to ignore the wrong done to him, repair the wall, and continue to flood his field again. The man did as the pastor advised. The following day, however, the neighbor had once again drained the man's water to his own field.

After three days of this, the man in a rage went again to his pastor and asked what he should do. After thinking for a moment, the pastor told the man to water his neighbor's field first, and then do his own. The man returned home and did as the pastor told him.

Three days later the neighbor came to the man, apologized for his conduct, and asked how he too could know the God of Christianity. A kind person knows that a little kindness goes a long way.

GROUP DISCUSSION AND SHARING

1. **Icebreaker** *(10-15 minutes)*
   Complete this sentence:
   - "A kind word said to me last week was . . ."

2. **Discussion** *(20-30 minutes)*
   Are the following quotes from this chapter on the mark or off the mark? Do you agree or disagree? Give reasons for your answer.
   - "When we speak of kindness, an internal experience will not suffice. We cannot hold kindness inside. We have to express it. We have to reach out and touch someone." (pg. 65)
   - " . . . some of the meanest people I know can quote the Bible forward and backward. They are familiar with biblical facts but have never translated the gospel into their lives. They know Christ came to bring good news, but they do not pass along that good news to others. Paul must have known similar people in First Church Ephesus. As a result he com-

manded them, and he commanded us to, 'be kind to one another.' " (pg. 67)

- " . . . whenever you sit next to people, you sit next to a problem." (pg. 68)
- "How do you usually handle interruptions? Do you view them as God's calling card or as a derailment?" (pg. 69)
- "Kindness—it may be a phone call asking someone how they are doing, a birthday card to a friend, a casserole for a neighbor who is sick. It is reaching out in a tangible way to care for someone—and it does wonders for the giver as well as the receiver." (pg. 71)

3. **Life Sharing** (*20-30 minutes*)
    Complete these sentences:
    - "A problem that has the best of me today is . . ."
    - "A tangible act of kindness I can perform tomorrow is . . ."

4. **Prayer** (*10-15 minutes*)
    As you pray today, have the leader mention each person by name and then two or three people briefly pray for that person. It goes like this:
    - "God, we lift before you John . . ."
      (And then two or three people pray for him).
    - Then the leader says,
      "God, we lift before you Peggy. . ."
      (And two or three people pray for her).

CHAPTER SIX

TEACH ONE ANOTHER

Let the word of Christ dwell in you richly;
teach and admonish one another in all wisdom;
and with gratitude in your hearts sing psalms, hymns,
and spiritual songs to God.
Colossians 3:16

Now when Jesus saw great crowds around him, he gave
orders to go over to the other side. A scribe then approached
and said, "Teacher, I will follow you wherever you go." And
Jesus said to him, "Foxes have holes, and birds of the air have
nests; but the Son of Man has nowhere to lay his head."
Matthew 8:18-20

And as he sat at dinner in the house,
many tax collectors and sinners came
and were sitting with him and his disciples.
When the Pharisees saw this, they said to his disciples,
"Why does your teacher eat with tax collectors
and sinners?"
Matthew 9:10-11

Then some of the scribes and Pharisees said to him,
"Teacher, we wish to see a sign from you."
Matthew 12:38-39

When they reached Capernaum, the collectors
of the temple tax came to Peter and said,
"Does your teacher not pay the temple tax?"
Matthew 17:24

Then someone came to him and said, "<u>Teacher</u>, what good
deed must I do to have eternal life?"
Matthew 19:16

On the first day of Unleavened Bread the disciples came to
Jesus, saying, "Where do you want us to make the
preparations for you to eat the Passover?" He said, "Go into
the city to a certain man, and say to him,
'The <u>Teacher</u> says, "My time is near; I will keep the Passover
at your house with my disciples." '
Matthew 26:17-18

THE MASTER TEACHER

Jesus was known as a great healer and a prodigious miracle worker,
but his contemporaries knew him best as "Teacher." Forty-nine
times—twelve times in Matthew, thirteen times in Mark, sixteen times
in Luke, eight times in John—his peers call him or refer to him as
"Teacher." Jesus even used the term to describe himself. After he
washed the disciples feet, he put on his robe, returned to the table and
said to them, "Do you know what I have done to you? You call me
Teacher and Lord—and you are right, for that is what I am. So if I, your
Lord and Teacher, have washed your feet, you also ought to wash one
another's feet" (John 13:12-14).

Jesus taught publicly in the open air, in homes, in synagogues,
and in the temple. He spoke authoritatively (Mark 1:22), and friends
and foes alike asked him questions about such things as the legality of
divorce (Mark 10:1-12), the penalties for adultery (John 7:53-8:11), the
requirement of Jewish tribute to Caesar (Mark 12:13-17), the doctrine
of the resurrection (Mark 12:18-27), and the relationship between sin
and sickness (John 9:2-3).

As we might pass along a prized possession or heirloom to
someone we love, Jesus passed along his teaching ministry to the disciples:

> Then before ascending to heaven, this master teacher
> sent forth his followers to teach. He said, "All authority
> in heaven and on earth has been given to me. Go there-

fore and make disciples of all nations, baptizing them in the name of the Father, and of the Son and of the Holy Spirit, and <u>teaching</u> them to obey everything I have commanded you. (Matthew 28:18-20)

As Jesus passed his teaching ministry to his disciples, the Apostle Paul passed it along to us! He wrote to the Colossians, and ultimately to us, instructing, "Let the word of Christ dwell in you richly; teach and admonish one another in all wisdom . . ." (Colossians 3:16).

Note a couple things from Paul's words to the Colossians. First, he said the word of Christ must dwell, or, literally, "keep house" —*enoikeito*—in us richly.

I once visited some married friends in Kansas City. They took me on a tour of their home. It was lovely, but I noticed a couple of things. I noticed the master bedroom was definitely her room. Frilly pillows. Feminine comforter. Pastel colors. That's where she "dwelt richly." That's where she "kept house." He, on the other hand, did not feel at home in that room. He did not dwell richly there. He did, however, dwell richly in his study. Sporting memorabilia accented the room. Masculine wallpaper hung on the walls. Walk into the study and you knew it was his study. Walk in the master bedroom and you knew it was her bedroom.

To dwell richly is to live comfortably in a particular space. That's what Christ wants to do with us. Christ wants to live comfortably in every room of our "house." Christ wants to be at home in our hearts and our minds. He wants his forgiveness, his mercy, his grace, his teachings to accent our lives.

It is from this rich dwelling place that we can teach one another. When Christ keeps house within us, we can reproduce what we have received. When we teach and admonish one another, presenting our learning, sharing our insights, challenging, supporting, questioning, guiding—we become communicators of Christ to each other. We may not hold court in a Sunday School class. We may not volunteer to lead the study in our small group, but we teach nonetheless. We teach by example and by a well-placed wise word here and there.

I think of my Friday noon small group. Bruce teaches me about the importance of missions. He has a highly developed social conscience. He has a heart for the poor. Mike teaches me about faith. Mike sees the cup as half-full. He looks at silver linings. He models a God-can-do spirit. Craig reminds me to keep my shoulder to the wheel. During studies he asks questions like, "On a scale of one to ten, with one being the lowest and ten the highest, where do you rank yourself on this particular virtue or habit? What do you want to do this week to make that better?" Bob teaches me about encouragement. He constantly looks for ways to compliment people. People love being in Bob's presence because he helps them feel better about themselves. As for me, I teach the guys about staying on task. I like things to begin and end on time. I keep the group moving and on schedule. In fact, I am so good with time, Bruce and his wife bought me a tie with little wrist watches in the design, saying it reminded them of me!

Even though we may not fill out lesson plans, and even though teaching may not be our spiritual gift, we teach every day of our lives. People see qualities in us that they admire, and they turn to us to learn how to possess those qualities themselves.

THE DESIRE TO GROW

Remember Peter Pan? Remember his song?

I won't grow up,
Not a penny will I pinch,
I will never grow a moustache,
or a fraction of an inch,
for growing up is awfuller
than all the awful things that ever were,
I will never grow up, never grow up,
never grow up, not me!

Peter led his young "disciples" in that song. With great gusto they proclaimed that they wanted to stay children forever. They could not imagine anything as bad as becoming an adult.

The Peter Pan Syndrome has made some inroads into the church. Every now and again we stumble upon a congregation like the one described in the Book of Hebrews. Listen to the author's frustration:

About this we have much to say that is hard to explain, since you have become dull in understanding. For though by this time you ought to be teachers, you need someone to teach you again the basic elements of the oracles of God. You need milk, not solid food; for everyone who lives on milk, being still an infant, is unskilled in the word of righteousness. But solid food is for the mature, for those whose faculties have been trained by practice to distinguish between good and evil. (Hebrews 5:11-14)

Obviously, this was a case of arrested development. Here were Christians who ought to have been teachers, modeling maturity in Christ, yet that was not the case. After many years they were still babes in the faith.

I vividly remember visiting the Duvall Home located an hour north of Orlando, Florida. This home, sponsored by the church and the state of Florida, cares for two hundred and fifty mentally challenged individuals. Some are mildly retarded, others severely. Residents range from infants to eighty-year-olds. On the day we visited, I met a woman who was celebrating her thirty-third birthday but had the mental capacity of a ten-year-old. She had birthday cards strewn over her bed and was most excited about the birthday cake she was going to receive later in the day. It happened that her name was the same as my daughter's: "Jenny."

Though grateful for the quality of care she and others were receiving at Duvall, I found myself feeling sad. I thought back to when my Jenny was an infant and a toddler and a pre-schooler. I remembered how much I loved those years, and I still recall the funny things she said as a little girl. In fact, we still have some "Jennyisms" that we share as a family. Some of her childhood sayings were cute and funny, but if my Jenny had grown into womanhood and continued saying the same things as the Jenny living in the Duvall Home, my joy would have turned to sorrow. As much as I loved her as a two-year-old, four-year-old, and ten-year-old, I love her even more now as a twenty-two-year old. I am thankful that she has grown mentally, socially, emotionally, spiritually, and physically over the years.

Feeling great grief for the arrested development of his readers, the author of Hebrews encouraged them to grow:

Therefore let us go on toward perfection, leaving behind the basic teaching about Christ, not laying again the foundation: repentance from dead works and faith toward God, instruction about baptisms, laying on of hands, resurrection of the dead, and eternal judgment. And we will do this, if God permits. (Hebrews 1:1-3)

I am reminded of a letter John Wesley was reported to have received. The letter stated, "The Lord has directed me to write you. Mr. Wesley, even though you know both Greek and Hebrew, the Lord can do without your book learnin'."

Wesley wrote back, "Your letter was superfluous. I already know the Lord can do without my learnin'. And while the Lord does not direct me to tell you, yet I wish to say on my own that the Lord does not need your ignorance either."

Indeed, God does not. Having mastered the basics of the faith, God wants us to grow in our faith. Most people I meet are hungry for spiritual growth. In a *Better Homes and Gardens* questionnaire, eighty percent of the respondents said that what they want most from a religious organization is spiritual growth.[1] Another study indicated that the top priority of Christians is "concentrating on the spiritual growth of one's family and self."[2]

The desire to grow, after all, is deeply implanted in the American psyche. William Ophuls says, "Growth is the secular religion of American society."[3] We live in a nation of seminars, books on tape, and self-help strategies. And who has implanted the desire to grow in our psyche? God.

Of course, we may not grow in the way God intended us to grow. We may grow like Alice-in-Wonderland. Remember her conversation with Dormouse?

> "I wish you wouldn't squeeze so," said the Dormouse, who was sitting next to her. "I can hardly breathe."
>
> "I can't help it," said Alice very meekly: "I'm growing."
>
> "You've no right to grow here," said the Dormouse.
>
> "Don't talk nonsense," said Alice more boldly: "You know you're growing too."
>
> "Yes, but I grow at a reasonable pace," said the Dormouse, "not in that ridiculous fashion."[4]

Some of us grow "ridiculously." We do not grow in ways God intended us to grow. If we place God at the center of our growth, however, the end product will be remarkable, not ridiculous. C. S. Lewis put it well. In very picturesque language he wrote,

Imagine yourself as a living house. God comes in to rebuild that house. At first, perhaps, you can understand what He is doing. He is getting the drains right and stopping the leaks in the roof and so on: you knew that those jobs needed doing and so you are not surprised. But presently He starts knocking the house about in a way that hurts abominably and does not seem to make sense. What on earth is He up to? The explanation is that He is building quite a different house from the one you thought of—throwing out a new wing here, putting on an extra floor there, running up towers, making courtyards. You thought you were going to be made into a decent looking cottage: but He is building a palace. He intends to come and live in it Himself.

The command *Be ye perfect* is not idealistic gas. Nor is it a command to do the impossible. He is going to make us into creatures that can obey that command. He said (in the Bible) that we were "gods" and He is going to make good His words. If we let Him—for we can prevent Him, if we choose—He will make the feeblest and filthiest of us into a god or goddess, dazzling, radiant, immortal creature, pulsating all through with energy and joy and wisdom and love as we cannot now imagine, a bright stainless mirror which reflects back to God perfectly (though, of course, on a smaller scale) His own boundless power and delight and goodness. The process will be long and in parts very painful; but that is what we are in for. Nothing less. He meant what He said.[5]

Alan Jones likened the process of spiritual growth to that of lobsters.[6] Like lobsters that grow too big for their shells and have to burst out of them and face the heat of the sun and the sting of the brine, exposing tender flesh to the elements, we may find our process hard to bear. Like heat and light, it takes getting used to.

When Jesus asked the paralytic man at the Pool of Bethesda, "Do you want to be made well?" (John 5:6), the paralytic dared to answer, "Yes." God asks us the same question: "Do you want to be made well? Do you want to change and grow and experience all that entails?"

Of course, you would not be reading this book if your answer was no. You would not be in a small group if your answer was no. The fact that you are reading this book and have joined a group show your desire to grow and change and learn all you can about yourself, others, and God. People in the group can teach you some things about God and relationships that you cannot learn anywhere else. And you have some valuable insights and ways of doing things that you can teach others.

THE DESIRE TO TEACH

So, you have a desire to grow. Your desire to teach, however, may be another matter. In this regard, you are not alone. We may want to grow, but not necessarily teach. Our reasons are many. First, we may not want to teach because we feel INADEQUATE for the job. With so much still to learn ourselves, how could we possibly begin to teach others? Of course, feeling inadequate puts us in good company. "I yam, what I yam," Popeye says, and by the grace of God, we are what we are—and what we are is inadequate. Inadequacy is a fact of life. "We're all ordinary people," G. K. Chesterton said, "and it's the extraordinary people who know it."[7]

Ninety percent of all clergy know it. I am not saying that ninety percent of all clergy are extraordinary. Rather, I am saying that, in a recent survey, ninety percent of all clergy reported feeling inadequately trained for ministry.[8] Feeling inadequate, however, is good news, not bad! If we are in a position where we feel inadequate for the task, such knowledge leaves room for God to operate in us and through us. Feeling inadequate is a prelude to God's power! Feeling inadequate places us in the best possible position for God to work!

I think of all the times as a parent I have prayed, "God, I do not know how to deal with this teenager. Help me. I'm losing patience." I think of all the times I have stood in the pulpit thinking, "This sermon is really bad. I don't even like it, let alone the poor people who are about to hear it. Do something with it that I haven't been able to do myself." I think of all the times in counseling sessions when I have quietly said, "God, I do not know what to say to this person or how to help. Bail me out!" I think of all the times as a husband when I have prayed, "God, how does this woman ever stay with me? I come up short in so many ways." Yet, in the midst of all those situations the one constant has been God and God's power. Living as a Christian is a lot like driving beyond one's headlights. Even though we cannot see beyond our limited range, we trust that God will meet us in our points of weakness.

* * *

The second reason we may hesitate to teach is due to FEAR. In a cartoon I saw years ago, a speaker was being introduced, and as the introduction was in progress, people were walking out of the hall. The man giving the introduction looked at the people leaving and said, "I see our speaker needs no introduction . . ."

We do not want to turn people away. We do not want to bore people, and we fear we may do that very thing. We fear we may "blow it." As fears go, speaking in front of others is our number one fear. Many people would rather sit in a room of snakes than get up in front of people, and since we often associate teaching with public speaking, we say, "Pass. Teaching is not for me. Get someone who is better on his or her feet."

Fortunately, much of good teaching comes from modeling. In small groups, God calls us to be spiritual friends, rather than spiritual directors to one another. In spiritual direction, the relationship is not one of equals: There is a director and a directee. Barry Woodbridge puts it well:

> For me, it is much easier to be a "spiritual director" than a spiritual friend. As a spiritual director, I have a professional role that defines what I speak about. Much of the time that role is to insure we keep to the topic of what is happening in the other person's prayer life . . . But spiritual direction is much more one-sided than spiritual friendship. As a spiritual director, I help keep others accountable to their vision of the Lord and the Lord's vision of them. My own growth does not enter the picture nearly as much as in spiritual friendship, where the relationship is meant to be reciprocal.[9]

As spiritual friends, we serve as guardians of one another's spirits. We pledge to help one another grow. We teach one another by sharing our experiences and insights. In small groups, teaching is not just leading the study for the evening; it is sharing with our fellow travelers where we have found bread.

* * *

The third reason we may hesitate to teach is due to the HOR-ROR STORIES we have heard from others. Here, for example, is a test that was administered to elementary school teachers at the teaching center in Marshall, Minnesota. The teachers were to answer each question "Yes" or "No" and analyze their score at the end:

HAVE YOU BEEN TEACHING TOO LONG?
Do you murmur "no cuts" when a shopper squeezes ahead of you in a checkout line?
Do you move your dinner partner's glass away from the edge of the table?
Do you say everything twice? I mean, do you repeat everything?
Do you ask if anyone needs to go to the bathroom as you enter a theater with a group of friends?
Do you hand a tissue to anyone who sneezes?
Do you refer to "snack time" instead of "happy hour?"
Do you ask guests if they have remembered their scarves and mittens as they leave your home?
Do you say, "I like the way you did that" to the mechanic who repairs your car?
Do you fold your spouse's fingers over coins as you hand him/her the money at a toll booth?
Do you sing the "Alphabet Song" to yourself as you look up a number in the phone book?
Do you ask a quiet person at a party if he/she has something to share with the group?

If you answered *yes* to more than two of the above, you are hooked on teaching. If you answered *yes* to more than one half of the questions, you are probably beginning to think about retirement. If you answered *yes* to more than ten, you'll always be a teacher, retired or not!

Some of us may feel as if we have been teaching too long after just one hour! And we have all heard horror stories of unruly children, unresponsive adults, uninterested parents, and unappealing teaching conditions. However, before letting these stories overshadow the great rewards of teaching, listen to the words of John W. Schlatter:

> I am a Teacher.
> I was born the first moment that a question leaped from the mouth of a child.
> I have been many people in many places.
> I am Socrates exciting the youth of Athens to discover new ideas through the use of questions.
> I am Anne Sullivan tapping out the secrets of the universe into the outstretched hand of Helen Keller.
> I am Aesop and Hans Christian Andersen revealing truth through countless stories.
> I am Marva Collins fighting for every child's right to an education.
> I am Mary McCleod Bethune building a great college for my people, using orange crates for desks.
> And I am Bel Kaufman struggling to go *Up The Down Staircase.*
> The names of those who have practiced my profession ring like a hall of fame for humanity . . . Booker T. Washington, Buddha, Confucius, Ralph Waldo Emerson, Leo Buscaglia, Moses and Jesus.
> I am also those whose names and faces have long been forgotten but whose lessons and character will always be remembered in the accomplishments of their students.
> I am a paradox. I speak the loudest when I listen the most. My greatest gifts are in what I am willing to appreciatively receive from my students.
> Material wealth is not one of my goals, but I am a full-time treasure seeker in my quest for new opportunities for my students to use their talents and in my constant search for those talents that sometimes lie buried in self-defeat.
> I am the most fortunate of all who labor.
> A doctor is allowed to usher life into the world in one magic moment. I am allowed to see that life is reborn each day with new questions, ideas and friendships.

An architect knows that if he builds with care, his structure may stand for centuries. A teacher knows that if he builds with love and truth, what he builds will last forever.

I am a warrior, daily doing battle against peer pressure, negativity, fear, conformity, prejudice, ignorance and apathy. But I have great allies: Intelligence, Curiosity, Parental Support, Individuality, Creativity, Faith, Love and Laughter all rush to my banner with indomitable support.

And so I have a past that is rich in memories. I have a present that is challenging, adventurous and fun because I am allowed o spend my days with the future.

I am a teacher . . . and I thank God for it every day.[10]

So are each one of us teachers. Jesus has enrolled us in this noble profession: "Go therefore and make disciples of all nations, baptizing them in the name of the Father, and of the Son, and of the Holy Spirit, *teaching* them to observe all that I have commanded you."

In Robert Bolt's play *A Man for All Seasons*, Sir Thomas More urges a restless underling to become a fine teacher. "And if I was, who would know it?" asks the ambitious young man.

Sir Thomas More answers, "You, your pupils, your friends, God. Not a bad public, that."

'Not a bad public at all!

GROUP DISCUSSION AND SHARING

1.   **Icebreaker** (10-15 *minutes*)
     • Who was your favorite elementary school teacher?
     • Who was your least favorite?

2.   **Discussion** (15-20 *minutes*)
     • Discuss this chapter. What did you like? What was a new insight? What would you challenge?
     • What do you hope you are teaching others? What do you fear you are teaching others?

3. **Application** *(15-20 minutes)*
    - Take a few minutes to write down the names of everyone in your group, and what each person has to teach you.
    - After the list is complete, go around the circle mentioning each member by name, and share what each person would like to learn from that member.

4. **Life Sharing** *(15-20 minutes)*
    - How can the group be praying for you in the days ahead?

5. **Prayer** *(5-10 minutes)*

CHAPTER SEVEN

LIVE IN HARMONY
WITH ONE ANOTHER

Finally, all of you, live in harmony with one another;
be sympathetic, love as brothers,
be compassionate and humble.
1 Peter 3:8 NIV

B rian Buhler tells a fictitious story of three men who were born blind but who had been miraculously healed by Jesus.[1] The three heard about one another and decided to get together to celebrate their unity in Christ and to exchange testimonies. After the men introduced themselves and exchanged warm embraces, one man began telling his story.

Bartimaeus said, "Gentlemen, let me go first. I cannot wait to tell you what Jesus did for me. I was outside the city of Jericho when Jesus walked by, surrounded by a mob of people. I cried out, 'Son of David! Son of David! Have mercy on me!' and Jesus stopped. The crowd quieted down. He asked me the most unusual question. He asked, 'What do you want me to do for you?' I said, 'Rabbi, I want to see.' He said, 'Go. Your faith has made you well.' Gentlemen, at that moment, instantaneously I could see. I was healed. As a result, I have come to this conclusion: When it comes to healing blind people, Jesus uses our faith and his word, and that equals healing."

The other two shook their heads and frowned. They obviously disagreed with Bartimaeus' conclusion. Unable to keep quiet, the man from Bethsaida spoke up. He said, "Gentlemen, my story of how Christ touched me isn't anything like that. Jesus took me out of the city, and he spit directly in my eyes. Then he touched my eyes with his hands. I was expecting an instantaneous healing like yours, Bartimaeus, but when I opened my eyes, it was awful. I saw men as trees walking. Everything was a blur. I thought, 'If this is what it is like to be healed by Jesus, he's not much of a healer.' Then Jesus repeated the procedure. He spit in my eyes again and touched me again. Gentlemen, the second time I opened my eyes, I could see. As a result, I am convinced that when Jesus heals blind people, he uses spit, and it's always in two stages."

By this time, the third man was red in the face. He said, "Gentlemen, I would seriously doubt the validity of both your conclusions. When Jesus healed me, he used saliva all right. But he did not spit in my face. Instead, he spit in the ground, and he took the saliva and the dirt and made mud packs and put mud packs on my eyes. It was uncomfortable and somewhat disgusting. Then he told me to go to the pool of Siloam and commanded me to wash the mud out in the pool. As I washed it out, I could see instantly. As a result, I am convinced that when Jesus heals blind people, he uses mud and the holy waters of the pool of Siloam."

The three men argued with one another well into the night and went away divided on the matter of Jesus and healing. In the days that followed they formed three denominations—the Mudites, the Spitites, and the Faithites. The Mudites made mud their sacrament of healing, the Spitites made saliva their sacrament, and the Faithites assigned no special sacrament at all to healing, believing that faith in Christ's word was all that was necessary to be made well.

Though fictional, Buhler's story strikes close to home. Even though the Apostle Peter encourages us to "live in harmony with one another," it does not take much to divide God's people. Just ask comedian Emo Philips. He tells the following story:

> In conversation with a person I had recently met, I asked, "Are you Protestant or Catholic?"
>
> My new acquaintance replied, "Protestant."
>
> I said, "Me, too! What franchise?"
>
> He answered, "Baptist."
>
> "Me, too!" I said. "Northern Baptist or Southern Baptist?"
>
> "Northern Baptist," he replied.
>
> "Me, too!" I shouted.
>
> "We continued back and forth. Finally I asked, "Northern conservative fundamentalist Baptist, Great Lakes Region Council of 1879 or Northern conservative fundamentalist Baptist, Great Lakes Region Council of 1912?"

He replied, "Northern conservative fundamentalist Baptist, Great Lakes Region Council of 1912."
I said, "Die, heretic!"[2]

This fictional account is a far cry from the words of the great
Lutheran reformer Philip Melancthon who proclaimed, "In the essentials, unity; in the nonessentials, liberty; in all things, charity." Unfortunately, the two northern conservative fundamentalist Great Lakes
Baptists considered *everything* essential. There were no gray areas or
places where they could disagree in love. Their attitudes toward one
another left much to be desired, and their interaction with one another
was a far cry from Jesus' prayer on the night of his arrest.

THE GIFT OF UNITY

Consider the setting of Jesus' prayer in that Upper Room. He
was surrounded by his disciples—the ones with proud hearts and for-
merly dirty feet. He began to pray. He did not invite the disciples to
participate in the prayer, but he did want them to listen. In this prayer,
his longest prayer recorded in the Gospels, Jesus asked for three
things. With the cross facing him, he first prayed for himself:

> "Father, the hour has come; glorify your Son so that the
> Son may glorify you, since you have given him author-
> ity over all people, to give eternal life to all whom you
> have given him." (John 17:1-2)

To "glorify" means to make known or to bring into the open. It
can refer to receiving human honor, but its chief use is to describe the
revelation of the character and presence of God in a person.[3] Jesus
wanted the disciples to see the glory of God in his death. He also
wanted to make sure that God would use his resurrection to let people
know he was who he said he was.
Second, Jesus prayed for his disciples:

> "I am asking on their behalf; I am not asking on behalf
> of the world, but on behalf of those whom you gave me,
> because they are yours . . . Holy Father, protect them in
> your name that you have given me, so that they may be
> one, as we are one . . . I am not asking you to take them

out of the world, but I ask you to protect them from the
evil one." (John 17:9; 11b; 15)

In this prayer, the disciples got to hear what Jesus thought of
them. In a few hours Jesus would be arrested and they would scatter.
But that is not what Jesus saw as he prayed: he saw what they would
be like after the resurrection. He saw how courageous they would
be—after the resurrection. He saw how faithful they would be—after
the resurrection. He saw how much they would understand—after the
resurrection. After the resurrection, they would know he had come
from God. After the resurrection, they would believe his word.

Jesus focused on their potential and not their shortcomings.
And what did he ask on their behalf? That they might be protected,
that they might be immersed in the truth, and that they might be one,
as he was one with God who sent him.

Catherine Oliver, our congregation's Director of Christian
Education, illustrated this oneness at a Holy Week service. Preaching
on the importance of "oneness" with Christ, she shared what it was
like to be pregnant with each of her daughters. She said, "Without a
sonogram, I could not see them, but I knew they were there! I felt their
movements, their kicks, their constant, rhythmic hiccups all hours of
the night. I also knew that, even though they were separate, we were
also one. We had separate heart beats, but my girls depended on my
heart beating to survive."

If Jesus had been a female, or if there had been female disciples
among the twelve, he might have shared a similar pregnancy illustration to help the disciples better understand this oneness. Even though
separate, Jesus was praying that these disciples' hearts would beat in
the same rhythm, the same harmony, the same love as beat between
his heart and God's heart.

Finally, after praying for himself and his disciples, Jesus prayed
for you and me:

"I ask not only on behalf of these, but also on behalf of
those who will believe in me through their word, that
they may all be one." (John 17:20)

In these words, Jesus prayed for those who through the ages
who would come to believe the message of the disciples. He prayed beyond the twelve disciples . . . for Dick Meyer, who would believe because of Paul's writings; for those believers in Detroit and Denver and

Dayton and Durham who would come to believe in him because of the word of Matthew, Mark, Luke, and John; for you and the other members of your small group. He had you and me on his heart and mind the night of his arrest. He prayed that we would be with him in glory and that we would all be one. He prayed not for a unity of administration or organization but for a unity of relationship.

The Biblical commentator William Barclay writes,

> It will never be that Christians will organize their Churches all in the same way. It will never be that they will worship God all in the same way. It will never even be that they will all believe precisely and exactly the same things. But the Christian unity is a unity which transcends all these differences, and joins people together in love. The cause of Christian unity at the present time, and indeed through all of history, has been injured and violated and hindered, because people loved their own ecclesiastical organizations, people loved their own creeds, people loved their own ritual, more than they loved each other. If we really loved each other and really loved Christ, no one would ever be excluded from any Church, and no Church would ever exclude any one who is Christ's disciple.[4]

I have seen this kind of unity in love over and over again. I remember an Episcopal church where, during the sacrament of the Lord's Supper, the celebrant said, "This is not an Episcopal table, this is Christ's table and all who confess Jesus are invited to participate in this holy meal." Being a Presbyterian, I did not feel excluded.

I saw unified love in action during a church building program. One of the "tribal chieftains" of the congregation was dead set against the idea of building. He would get red in the face discussing it. Yet, when the vote was cast and the decision was made to build, he came forward to make the first public pledge. He said, "This is what the body of Christ has chosen to do, and I'm going along."

I see unity in action most every Sunday morning in our congregation. We have three distinct worship services: an early-bird golden oldie "hymns-we-love-to-sing" service; a contemporary service with drums, guitar, and worship team; and a traditional service with choir and liturgy. What binds us together is our love for Christ. Traditional worship or contemporary worship may not be our thing, but we see its value for others. When it comes to worship, we celebrate our unity and diversity as people of God.

In 1994 superstar tenors Jose Carreras, Placido Domingo, and Luciano Pavarotti performed together in Los Angeles. A reporter tried to press the issue of competitiveness among the three men.

"You have to put all of your concentration into opening your heart to the music," was Domingo's response. "You can't be rivals when you're together making music."

That is also true in a small group. When we live in harmony, we can make beautiful music together.

THE CHALLENGE OF UNITY

Of course, living in harmony with one another presents a great challenge. The German philosopher Schopenhauer compared the human race to a bunch of porcupines huddling together on a cold winter's night. He observed, "The colder it gets outside, the more we huddle together for warmth; but the closer we get to one another, the more we hurt one another with our sharp quills."[5]

I think of the congregation I serve. We have men and women, young and old, Republicans and dyed-in-the-wool Democrats, people with Ph.D.s and people who quit school, life-long residents and Welcome Wagon prospects. We have Northerners and Southerners, people who love the Florida Gators and people who love the Florida State Seminoles, people who are tone-deaf and people who teach music. We have people who home-school and people who believe in public schools, people who love rock-and-roll and folk who love Rachmaninoff. There is tremendous diversity in our congregation. Many of us have little in common and what binds us together can only be something supernatural. We find our unity through our connection in Christ. If it were not for him, we would fly apart.

Apparently, that was the case in a congregation in a small town in Tennessee. They flew apart rather than staying together. Their place of worship had a sign in front that read, "LEFT FOOT BAPTIST CHURCH." It seems a number of years ago, there had been a split in this local congregation that practiced foot-washing. An argument had broken out over which foot should be washed first. The group insisting on the left foot taking precedence finally withdrew and split off to organize its own church and named its congregation accordingly!

A division like that might be funny if it were not so tragic, and small groups are not immune from such a split. Even though you may have much in common with those in your group, there are issues upon which you may never see eye-to-eye. Some will be "left foot" issues: Should we serve refreshments or not? Should we meet in the same place every week or rotate homes? Should we pray at the beginning or just at the end of the group? Some will be very weighty issues: Can we stay together after this break of confidence? Can pro-life and pro-choice people co-exist? Do I have anything in common with someone half my age or twice my age? Can we of different faith traditions learn to get along? Every small group faces the same challenge. Can our oneness in Christ hold us together when we are tempted to split apart?

THE BEAUTY OF UNITY

If that oneness can hold us together, we may experience something extraordinary. We may experience Liberal Democrats or Right Wing Republicans as loveable people—even if they do hold "strange" ideas. We might discover that people of different ethnic or racial backgrounds are more like us than they are different from us. We might discover that we do not have all the answers and that life is more complicated than we had first thought. We might learn how to hold some things more loosely and actually come to believe less things. We might discover that people can be more important than principles. In other words, we may experience the beauty of authentic Christian community, where Christ holds us together and teaches us to love and embrace those who differ from us.

It is a rare commodity—this kind of community—but you may be fortunate enough to experience it. And if you do, it will speak volumes to those outside your group. When others who are not in your group see or hear what you are experiencing, they will want what you have: a taste of heaven on earth.

Joseph Aldrich points to four signposts that draw people to Christ: love, unity, good works, and hope.[6] When people observe and sense these signposts, they sense that something uniquely divine is at work. Genuine unity apparently is such a rare commodity that when followers of Christ exhibit it, those outside Christ conclude that something out of the ordinary, something supernatural, must be taking place. Jesus certainly alluded to that fact when he prayed in the Upper Room:

> "As you, Father, are in me and I am in you, may they also be in us, so *that the world may believe that you have sent me.* The glory that you have given me I have given them, so that they may be one, as we are one, I in them and you in me, that they may be completely one, *so that the world may know that you have sent me and have loved them even as you have loved me."* (John 17:21-23)

According to Jesus, the unity we display among ourselves will draw those in "the world" to him. Unity will focus their attention in the right direction.

Also note that Jesus prays for unity, not uniformity. Christians do not have to look, think, dress, and act alike. The church is not an assembly line producing only Fords or Chevys. God does not seek a collection of robots. Rather, biblical unity produces a healthy diversity that is essential for beauty and authenticity.[7] The Holy Spirit has endowed the people of God with an amazing diversity of gifts, abilities, talents, and cultural distinctiveness. God seeks people with varying personalities, talents, and styles who are unified in purpose and will work toward the common good. This rich tapestry of diversity and unity draws people to God. The opposite, however, is also true. When diversity and unity are missing, outsiders have little interest in discovering more about Christ.

For example, one of the misperceptions about becoming a Christian goes something like this: "If you commit your life to following Jesus Christ, you can take your freedom, your individuality, your sense of adventure, and kiss them all goodbye. After all, when you become a Christian, you're signing up to join a bunch of lobotomized, look-alike, act-alike losers who have nothing better to do with their lives."[8]

Many outside the faith see Christians as lacking the sparkle of true vitality. They see Christians as cult-like zombies stripped of their individuality. In some places that may be true, but when the Spirit is present, diversity is present. E. Stanley Jones had the capacity to put profound truths into brief, pithy statements, which made him such a powerful communicator of the gospel. One of his favorite statements was, "To be most Christian is to be most natural."[9] Indeed it is. To be most Christian is to allow the Spirit to help us become what we are naturally and uniquely intended by God to be. Think of the Church as a great orchestra. Violins. Tubas. Cellos. French Horns. Piccolos. Flutes. Drums. If we were all violins or tubas, the sound would not be as rich or inspiring. Not only that, if all the piccolos tried to be tubas, what a tragedy that would be!

THE DANGER OF UNITY

Any discussion of unity would not be complete without mentioning a couple of dangers. The desire for unity can squash healthy dissent, and the power of unity can be used for evil as well as good.

Psychologists Martin Bolt and David Myers call this negative aspect "groupthink."[10] "Groupthink" flourishes when the desire to maintain group harmony leads to a suppression of dissent. Bolt and Myers use this example of a rapidly growing church, planning to construct an elaborate new facility, to make their point:

> Everyone seems to be on board. No one raises any questions about the architectural drawings. One church council member, a middle-aged real estate broker, has some questions about the congregation's ability to fund the project, but he keeps those questions to himself because he does not want to dampen the enthusiasm. When he shares his concern privately with another member of the council, he is told, "You lack faith." He thinks maybe the council member is right. Maybe he does not have enough faith. After all, no one else seems to be concerned about paying for this ambitious project. Inspired by a dynamic young pastor, and certain the new building will attract new members, the council votes unanimously to go ahead with the project. Bonds are sold, and a sizeable debt is incurred. Two years later, the same council members find it impossible to service the debt. Disaster looms.

What happened? "Groupthink." Critical judgment, the weighing of pros and cons, was suspended in an attempt to maintain group consensus. The fear of conflict led to blind conformity.

The other danger of unity relates to power. Unity produces strength; disunity produces weakness. United we stand, divided we fall. All that is well and good when the power that unity generates is used for good. But when the power of unity is used for evil, it is another story, as illustrated in the classic story of The Tower of Babel. The story begins with a people unified and working in harmony. "Now the whole earth had one language and the same words" (Genesis 11:1). They had discovered how to use brick and mortar, and they set out to build a tower that would reach into the heavens. They said,

> "Come, let us build ourselves a city and a tower with its top in the heavens, and let us make a name for our-selves; otherwise we shall be scattered abroad upon the face of the earth." (Genesis 11:4)

Their sin was pride. They wanted to make a name for themselves. They wanted to build a memorial to themselves, a symbolic assault on heaven in defiance of God. God responded swiftly,

> "Look, they are one people, and they have all one language; and this is only the beginning of what they will do; nothing that they propose to do will now be impossible for them. Come, let us go down, and confuse their language there, so that they will not understand one another's speech." (Genesis 11:6-7)

Working together, humans have found cures for life-threatening diseases, split atoms, traveled to far-away places, and stemmed the tides of floods. On the other hand, humans working together have also produced Nazi Germany, the Holocaust, and world-wide terrorism. Unified power can become overwhelming. Unity in itself is not good. Unity is good only when it is used for good.

People working in harmony in groups have done wonderful things: served in soup kitchens, built Habitat for Humanity houses, sponsored Third World children. People working in harmony in groups have also split churches, driven away competent clergy, and caused needless heartache and pain for the larger community. How will your group will use the power of unity?

THREE PRACTICES FOR DIFFUSING DISUNITY

A young rabbi was dismayed to find a serious quarrel among members of his new congregation. The quarrel took up all the congregation's energy. During Friday services, half the participants stood up during one part of the proceedings while half remained seated. All decorum was lost as each side shouted at the other side to conform. Members of each group insisted that theirs was the correct tradition. Seeking guidance, the young rabbi took a representative from each side to visit the synagogue's founder, a ninety-nine-year-old rabbi living in a nursing home.

"Rabbi, isn't it true that the tradition was always for the people to stand at this point in the service?" inquired the man from the standing-up side.

"No, that was not the tradition," the old man replied.

"Then it is true the tradition is for people to stay seated?" asked the sitting-down representative.

"No," the rabbi said, "that was not the tradition."

"But, rabbi," cried the young rabbi, "what we have now is complete chaos; half the people stand and shout, while the others sit and scream."

"Ah," said the old man. "THAT was the tradition."

● PRACTICE ONE: *CLASP*

We can smile at this story, but we know that conflict is inevitable. It certainly was in the Scriptures. In fact, much of the New Testament was written to address conflicts in churches. Differences of opinion happen whenever two or more people come together for any purpose. It will certainly arise in your small group. People will have different ideas on what to study, how to pray, what the proper interpretation of a Bible passage or current event should be, how the group should use its time.

When these conflicts arise, practice the CLASP method of dealing with them:

Calm down.
Lower your voice.
Acknowledge the other person's position.
State your position.
Propose a solution that takes into consideration the peace and the unity of the group.

● PRACTICE TWO: *Claim Christ as common ground.*

Dr. Newman Hall wrote a book entitled *Come to Jesus* that was criticized rather vociferously by another pastor. Hall sat down and wrote a vehement response to the criticism. Before mailing the letter to his critic, however, Hall took it to Charles Spurgeon, the great London minister, for his opinion. Spurgeon read it carefully, handed it back, saying, "It just lacks one thing." After a pause, Spurgeon continued, "Underneath your signature you ought to write the words, 'Author of *Come to Jesus.'"*

Hall tore the letter to shreds.[11]

In a small group, when people do not see eye-to-eye, it helps "to come to Jesus." It helps to see one another through Christ's eyes and to ask, "What might Jesus say or do in this situation? If Jesus were here, how do you suppose he would handle his situation or this person?"

● PRACTICE THREE: *Adopt an attitude of grace.*

A third way to diffuse disunity is to make grace your overall attitude. Ken Blanchard, author of *The One-Minute Manager,* had a conversation with his guru, Peter Drucker, one of the great thinkers of the world. Blanchard asked him, "Why are you a Christian?"

Drucker answered, "There is no better deal."

Blanchard clarified, "What do you mean?"

Drucker said, "Who else has grace?"[12]

An overall attitude of grace means giving others some wiggle room. Showing some tolerance. Letting some things slide. Remember the counsel of Philip Melancthon: "In the essentials, unity; in the nonessentials, liberty; in all things, charity."

The challenge in any small group is learning how to disagree without being disagreeable. May you meet that challenge in your group.

GROUP DISCUSSION AND SHARING

1. **Icebreaker** *(15-20 minutes)*
    - Since your group last met, when did you particularly feel "in tune" at work, home, or church?
    - When did you feel "out of tune?"

2.   **Discussion** *(20-30 minutes)*
     Comment on the following statements from the chapter:

     - "It will never be that Christians will organize their Churches all in the same way. It will never be that they will worship God all in the same way. It will never even be that they will all believe precisely and exactly the same things. But the Christian unity is a unity which transcends all these differences, and joins people together in love" (William Barclay). (pg. 91)

     - "The German philosopher Schopenhauer compared the human race to a bunch of porcupines huddling together on a cold winter's night. He observed, 'The colder it gets outside, the more we huddle together for warmth; but the closer we get to one another, the more we hurt one another with our sharp quills.' " (pg. 92)

     - "God seeks people with varying personalities, talents, styles who are unified in purpose and will work toward the common good. This rich tapestry of diversity and unity draws people to God. The opposite, however, is also true. When diversity and unity are missing, outsiders have little interest in discovering more about Christ." (pg 94)

     - "The challenge in any small group is learning how to disagree without being disagreeable." (pg 98)

3.   **Life Sharing** *(15-25 minutes)*
     Choose one or both of the sentence completions to share with your group:

     - A place where I need to guard against falling into "groupthink" is . . .

     - A place where I would like to sow some seeds of harmony is . . .

4.   **Prayer** *(10-15 minutes)*

     - How can the group be praying for you?

CHAPTER EIGHT

FORGIVE ONE ANOTHER

Be kind to one another, tenderhearted,
forgiving one another,
as God in Christ has forgiven you.
Ephesians 4:32

I cringe every time I think about it. I was twelve years old, living in Southern California, and I had my heart set on a swimming pool. My parents were divorced, and I lived with my mother who, like many single mothers, lived from paycheck to paycheck, trying to make ends meet. She worked as a secretary, and we lived in a modest two-bedroom apartment. My father was a vice-president of a savings-and-loan and was financially secure. When he remarried and purchased a large home in the foothills of Los Angeles, he told me that he would consider putting in a swimming pool in his backyard. I waited expectantly for that to happen. My Aunt Irene, his sister, had a pool in her backyard, and I swam there every chance I got.

Shortly after he moved into the house, he took me to look at pools. We visited three or four showrooms, even picked out the design we wanted, but he never got the pool. He gave me his reasons: (a) I was getting older and would not be spending as much time with him on weekends, and the pool would not get much use when I was gone; (b) It was quite an expense, and Aunt Irene said we could use her pool whenever we wanted to swim; (c) It cost too much to maintain.

The reasons made sense to him, but not to me, so I stopped speaking to him. I refused to visit him on weekends. When he would call, I would refuse to talk. For six months I did not communicate with my father. He had let me down, and I was not about to forgive him. Then baseball season started, and I needed a new baseball glove. The glove cost $55, which was quite a bit of money in 1960. I called him on the phone and told him about the glove. He asked me how much it cost. I told him. He said, "Let's go see it." We went to the sporting goods store, he bought the glove, and after six months of noncommunication, I started visiting him again. He never did put in a pool, but I now have one in my backyard. Every time I use it, I think of him and our argument!

BIBLICAL WORDS FOR FORGIVENESS

Forgiveness does not come easily for many of us. Pride, anger, bitterness, hurt feelings often get in the way. Some of us go to our graves with hurts, slights, offenses still burning in our bellies, yet forgiveness is at the heart of the Christian faith. Jesus not only cried out, "Father, forgive them; for they do not know what they do" at his crucifixion (Luke 23:34), but the Apostle Paul also instructed us to be a forgiving people. To his little congregation in Ephesus he wrote, "Be kind to one another, tenderhearted, forgiving one another, as God in Christ has forgiven you" (Ephesians 4:32).

Biblical authors used six different words, three Hebrew and three Greek, to express the nuances of forgiveness.[1]

The Hebrew words for forgiveness are:

kaphar, meaning "to cover." This word occurs only three times in the Old Testament [2] and conveys the idea of covering up sin or hiding it.

nasa, meaning "to bear, take away, lift up." This word, which appears fifteen times, has the notion of taking away guilt for the purpose of forgiveness.

sallach, the most common Hebrew word for forgiveness, appears twenty-five times and literally means "to send away, to let go." This word is always used of God's forgiveness of people, and never of person-to-person forgiveness.

The Greek words for forgiveness are:

charizomai, meaning "to deal graciously with."

apheimi, meaning "to send away or let go."

apolyo, meaning "to free or loose."

In his letter to the Ephesians, the Apostle Paul used *charizomai*, but all these Greek and Hebrew words taken together give a valuable understanding of forgiveness. Forgiveness includes not only the idea of pardon and the removal of guilt, but also the concept of abandoning of any claim we may have on the guilty person. As God let go of our trespasses, we are to let go of those who trespass against us.

OUR MODEL OF FORGIVENESS

None of this can come about, however, without a solid vertical connection to God. Of the 122 verses that contain the word "forgive" in the Bible, only eighteen percent deal with person-to-person, or "horizontal," forgiveness. The rest (eighty-two percent) are all in the context of God forgiving people, or "vertical forgiveness." And even in the verses dealing with horizontal forgiveness, 19 out of the 22 explicitly connect horizontal forgiveness with vertical forgiveness. This means that ninety-seven percent of the total verses dealing with forgiveness relate to vertical forgiveness. In other words, God's vertical forgiveness seems to go ahead of, and make possible, horizontal forgiveness.

That certainly is the point Jesus drives home in "The Parable of the Unforgiving Servant" (Matthew 18:21-22). One particular conversation prompted this parable. Peter asked Jesus, "If my brother keeps sinning against me, how often should I forgive him? Seven times?" Reading between the lines of the question, one wonders if Peter's brother Andrew was driving him up a wall. Peter appeared at the end of his rope. He had probably forgiven his brother a handful of times, but Andrew kept getting under Peter's skin. How many times was he supposed to let his little brother off the hook? "Is seven times enough?" he asked Jesus.

Peter was actually being magnanimous, for the going rate was three times. The Jews were instructed to forgive once, forgive twice, and a third time, but from then on, forget it. Peter, however, doubled the amount and added one for good measure. Surely, this standard of forgiveness would more than suffice.

Jesus answered, "No, old boy, not seven times, but seven times seventy!" In other words, forgive your brother an infinite number of times. Jesus did not mean, literally, "Forgive your brother or sister or spouse or neighbor 490 times, and when number 491 rolls around, quit." This is not a gospel of calculators but a gospel of grace. We are to be typified by a forgiving spirit, with forgiveness as a continual attitude in our lives.

Jesus then told Peter a parable (Matthew 18:23-35) about a man who owed ten thousand talents to his king. That was a whole lot of money! It would be the equivalent of ten million dollars in United States currency, and in that day, a man would make only about ten talents in his lifetime. When the king called him on the carpet and told him he needed to pay up, the guy said he did not have it but promised to pay it all back if he could just have more time. The king then turned to his aides and began discussing the possibility of selling this man, his wife, and children into slavery, and disposing of his personal property to recoup a small portion of the debt. When the man pleaded for mercy, the king did the incredible: He reached into his ledger, took hold of the man's account, and ripped it out. He then turned to the man and said, "I forgive the debt. Have a nice day!"

The response of the servant, however, was nothing less than repulsive. Within minutes he happened across a fellow who owed him twenty bucks. We expect him to be as gracious and merciful with the man as the king had been to him. Instead, he grabbed the man by the throat and demanded the money. When the man could not pay, the unforgiving servant had him thrown into prison. In other words, even though the king had shown the servant ten million dollars of mercy, the servant was unwilling to pass along just 1/500,000, or twenty dollars, of that mercy to another.

The point of the parable is clear: the debt to forgive others is ongoing because of the great debt forgiven us. Gratitude for the grace shown us is to be passed on. As God has forgiven us, we are to forgive others. Forgiveness is not an elective in Christianity. It is a required course.

The Apostle Paul picked up this same thought in his letter to the Ephesians: "Forgive one another, *as God in Christ has forgiven you.*" This does not mean we are to be as forgiving as our Aunt Mary, or Brother Bill, or Cousin Samantha—as forgiving as they may all be. The divine standard of forgiveness is much greater: We are to be as forgiving of one another as God is of us.

SOME BARRIERS TO FORGIVENESS

Forgiveness may be a required course in Christianity, but we find it difficult to pass the exams. Four things often trip us up on "forgiveness" exams.

- THE FIRST BARRIER: *Not accepting our own forgiveness.*

One of the ways we "flunk" the forgiveness exam is that we have trouble receiving the gracious forgiveness offered to us. That certainly was what tripped up the unforgiving servant. He was unable to let himself off the hook. One of the sadnesses of the parable is that the unforgiving servant thought he could pay off his debt. He thought he could earn his forgiveness. Even though he would have needed to work a hundred thousand years to pay off the debt, he said to the king, "Have patience with me, and I will pay you everything."

It happens to many of us. We hate to be in debt to anyone. At Christmas we feel awkward when someone gives us a hundred-dollar gift when we only spent twenty dollars on them. We want to stay on an even playing field. We cannot even receive a compliment. Someone says, "What a great dress!" and we respond with, "This old thing? I've had it for years." If someone buys our lunch, we say, "I'll get it next time." Over the years we have had such axioms as, "Never take anything from anyone; you've got to pull your own weight," drummed into our head. We feel as if we need to earn our forgiveness rather than simply accept it. Putting ourselves in the shoes of the unforgiving servant, it would take us one hundred thousand years to pay off the debt of Christ's forgiveness. If we could receive that forgiveness, if we could let ourselves off the hook, we would be able to let others off the hook as well.

- THE SECOND BARRIER: *Taking justice into our own hands.*

We also flunk the forgiveness exam because we try to take justice into our own hands. Instead of trusting God to balance the scales, we decide to do it ourselves. Like Archie Bunker, we think, "What's wrong with revenge? It's the perfect way to get even." So, we give someone the silent treatment or we treat them shabbily or we tell "ain't it awful" stories about them to others, all the while attempting to balance the scales. We want to inflict as much hurt on them as they have on us.

The problem with this, however, is that we wind up inflicting as much pain on ourselves as we do the other person. As a result, the scales never balance. Jesus described this dead-end process in the parable of the unforgiving servant. The punch line reads, "And in anger his lord handed him over to be tortured until he would pay his entire debt" (Matthew 18:34). The key word here is "tortured." It comes from a Greek word meaning "to torment." The warning of this parable is harsh and clear: If we do not forgive, we will be tormented, eaten up by our bitter, unforgiving spirit.

I am reminded of what a New York City physician discovered in his practice. He was re-reading some of his patients' case histories, and he discovered that seventy percent of his patients had one thing in common: Their case histories all revealed resentments. They carried hurts and bitterness that still bothered them. The physician claimed, "If my patients ever learned how to dispense forgiveness, I wouldn't need to dispense so many pills."

Norman Vincent Peale tells of a woman who came up to him with a blunt announcement: "I itch terribly. I've had it off and on for about three years, but it's particularly bad when I am in church. Look at my arm." The exposed arm showed nothing but a slight redness. He was curious why the itching was particularly noticeable when she came to church. They set up a counseling appointment and what emerged was a dark hatred of her sister.

She claimed that her older sister, executor of their father's estate, had defrauded her of her rightful inheritance. He reasoned that, because she was a long-time church member, the hatred was compounded with a sense of guilt when she came to church. She granted him permission to speak to her physician. The physician said, "This woman possibly has what we call an 'internal eczema.' She has been scratching herself on the inside and producing an outward pseudo-itching. I have a hunch that if she would drop the hatred, she might get over it. At least it's worth trying."

The doctor talked with the patient and gave her this warning: "You'll itch yourself into a breakdown if you do not change your sick thought pattern." The woman took her physician's advice. She forgave her sister, not without effort, and exorcised the hate, and the itching got less and less until it finally ceased altogether.[3]

When we are unwilling to forgive, who bears the pain? Jesus says we do, and medical science bears that out.

- THE THIRD BARRIER: *Not wanting to take the initiative.*

Another way we fail the forgiveness exam is that we wait for someone to ask for our forgiveness before we give it. How many times have we caught ourselves saying something like, "Forget it! I am not going to forgive that person until he admits he is wrong!"

That certainly was the case with me. I had been invited to celebrate my former congregation's fortieth anniversary. While celebrating their forty years of ministry, they were also going to kick off their building program. I almost did not go because I was carrying a grudge. Seven years earlier a key member of the building effort—a multimillionaire—had hurt me deeply. He had tried to use money to influence the congregation's choice of an architect, threatening that if they did not choose a particular architect, he would leave the church . . . which he did. After I left, he returned to the church and the congregation changed architectural firms. In actuality, the church was much more forgiving than I.

I told Trudy about the invitation. I told her I would love to go, but I could not go in good conscience and support the building program.

Trudy said, "How long do you want to carry a grudge? How long do you want to stay angry at this guy? Forgive him and move on!"

I said, "But he didn't ask for forgiveness!"

She responded, " Take the first step. Forgive him anyway."

The message of Jesus' story is that forgiveness is unconditional. Jesus' death and resurrection were not contingent upon our behavior; he did not wait for us to say, "We're sorry; we really blew it." Neither did he say to his disciple Peter, "Pete, forgive them seventy times seven, but only if they say they are sorry first."

This is in no way to downplay the importance of confession, of going to someone and actually saying, "I am truly sorry." Confession is good for the soul, but we need to remember that confession is the condition whereby forgiveness is *received* on the other end. As far as our end is concerned, the *giving* of forgiveness is to be unconditional.

● THE FOURTH BARRIER: *Not "feeling" like forgiving.*

We may also fail the forgiveness exam because we do not *feel* like forgiving the other person. That certainly was the case in one small group where a member of the group broke a confidence. Out of concern, this person shared with the pastor what a woman in the group had revealed the previous night. The problem was the woman did not want the pastor to have this information. The next time the group met, she confronted the person who had passed along the information. The offending person asked for forgiveness, saying, "I know I should have asked for permission first before sharing it with the pastoral staff. I have no excuse for what I did. Please forgive me." The offended woman, however, refused to forgive. In fact, the offended woman left the small group and never joined another group! She did not want anything to do with the person who had broken her trust. Forgiveness, however, has nothing to do with feelings. It has everything to do with obedience: "Forgive one another as God in Christ has forgiven you."

Harry Emerson Fosdick tells this appropriate story: When he was a little boy, he overheard a conversation between his father and mother at the breakfast table. He heard his dad say, "Tell Harry he can mow the grass today if he feels like it." As his father left, he heard him call back, "Tell Harry he better feel like it."

Forgiveness is a not a feeling; it is a command. Jesus' words to us are explicit: "Whenever you stand praying, forgive, if you have anything against anyone; so that your Father in heaven may also forgive you your trespasses" (Mark 11:25). He did not say, "Whenever you stand praying, if you feel like it, forgive." He simply said, "Forgive" whether you feel like it or not.

STEPS TO FORGIVENESS

So where do we begin? We know what we are to do, but how do we go about doing it? How do we get from point A (anger) to point B (forgiveness)? Here are some steps you can take.

● <u>STEP ONE</u>: *Remove the barriers.*

The first step to forgiveness begins with removing the barriers that keep us from experiencing God's grace and forgiveness in our lives. Listen to the lesson from one small boy:

> A brother and a sister spent a summer with their grandparents. One day the grandfather made a sling-shot and handed it to his grandson, saying, "Now, be careful with this and never shoot it at people or animals."
>
> "OK, Gramps," the boy promised, and he spent the next few days firing rocks at trees, cans, and other make-believe antagonists. Then one morning he spied, far across the pond, his grandmother's pet duck. Not really aiming, he let a rock fly. It arched through the air and hit the duck squarely in the head. The duck died. The little boy, fearing his grandparents' wrath, desperately searched for a place to hide the dead duck. Find-

ing the perfect place, he hid the duck under the pile of firewood near the barn. As he stood up, however, he spied his sister watching from the front porch.

"Lunch is ready, brotherrrrr," she said ever so sweetly.

"Oh no," he realized, "she saw everything." His spirit fell, and all through lunch he was silent. His food sat like lead in his stomach. He waited for his sister to expose his misdeed. She did not say a thing. She smiled at him and silently ate her sandwich.

Then grandmother spoke, "Sally, will you help me wash the dishes?"

"I'd be happy to Grandma, but Johnny told me he wanted to help in the kitchen today. Didn't you, Johnny?" Johnny considered a protest, but he sat there in grim silence realizing bad days were ahead.

The rest of the week was a nightmare for Johnny. He skipped a fishing trip so he could help make supper, and then he graciously let his sister lick the fudge pan. After many days of doing his sister's chores, he could take it no longer. "Grandma," he tearfully confessed, "I didn't mean to do it, but I killed your duck."

The grandmother said, "I know. I was standing at the window. I saw the whole thing. Because I love you, I forgave you, but I had to wait until you were ready to come to me and ask forgiveness. I wondered how long you would let your little sister keep you a slave."

The boy had to get over the barrier of FEAR. He hated to think what his grandmother might do to him when she discovered how her pet duck died.

Another barrier we need to remove is DENIAL. The Apostle John writes, "If we say we have no sin, we deceive ourselves, and the truth is not in us" (1 John 1:8). If we think we do not need forgiveness, we are in major denial.

A curious story springs from Frederick the Great. Frederick visited a prison in Potsdam where each prisoner he met made it very clear that he was an innocent person who had experienced a travesty of justice. Finally, Frederick came to a man who was hanging his head and looking down at the floor. When he was addressed, this man said, "Your Majesty, I am guilty and I deserve this punishment."

Quickly the king called the warden of the prison and instructed him to release this prisoner immediately. He said to the warden, "You must free him before he corrupts all the innocent people here!"

Many of us do not experience God's grace and forgiveness because we deny we have done anything wrong. We rationalize our behavior and say, "It's not really my fault. There were extenuating circumstances."

Think of all the news items you have seen where someone has claimed, "It's not my fault." A San Francisco city supervisor claimed he murdered a fellow supervisor and Mayor George Moscone because of eating junk food that made him act irrationally. A woman drove her car over her lover, claiming it was not her fault because she was suffering from PMS. The police in Los Angeles beat the motorist Rodney King before live television cameras. The jury acquitted the police of all but minor charges, deciding they were caught up in the mayhem of the moment and therefore not responsible for their actions.

It seems as if no one "sins" any more; there are always extenuating circumstances that explain our actions. I think of Dr. Karl Menninger's question: "Is no one responsible, or no one answerable for these acts . . . has no one committed any sins? Where indeed did sin go? What became of it?"[4]

A third barrier to experiencing God's grace and forgiveness is DELUSION. Delusion is denial's kissing cousin. Denial says, "I haven't really done anything wrong." Delusion says, "Sin is no big deal."

We battle the sun here in Florida. Skin cancer runs rampant. One must be sure to wear sun screen and protective clothing twelve months of the year. Those who grew up in the Florida sun often hear their dermatologist tell them later in life, "You have a skin melanoma caused by overexposure to the sun. If we do not remove it, that little spot will grow and spread cancer throughout your body."

Despite the danger, however, many in our state continue to worship the sun. They say, "It's no big deal. Exposure to the sun will not hurt me. I do not have to worry about getting skin cancer." Such thinking is delusional. The risk is real and great.

Sin is a lot like a little skin melanoma. It looks small, insignificant, but it can spread and drain our spiritual energy. If we think sin is no big deal, we are only fooling ourselves. Not only that, such an attitude short circuits the reception of forgiveness. And it follows that, if we think sin is no big deal, then forgiveness is no big deal. If we have not done "all that much," then we do not need to be forgiven of all that much.

A fourth barrier to experiencing God's grace and forgiveness is full DISCLOSURE. The Apostle John writes, "If we confess our sins, he who is faithful and just will forgive our sins and cleanse us from all unrighteousness" (1 John 1:9).

Did you catch the condition? *If* we confess, we will experience God's forgiveness. If not, we will not. When we confess, we disclose who we are. Some people, however, would rather drink a dill pickle milk shake than admit they are wrong. They refuse to come clean before God. I think of the conversation between Calvin and Hobbes:

> Calvin says to his imaginary playmate, Hobbes, "I feel bad that I called Susie names and hurt her feelings. I'm sorry I did it."
> "Maybe you should apologize," suggests Hobbes.
> Calvin ponders this for a moment and replies, "I keep hoping there's a less obvious solution."[5]

We all want a less obvious solution. As Mark Twain stated, "Confession is good for the soul, but bad for the reputation"—and the person hardest to face is ourselves. I have a theory. I think we hesitate to confess because we hate to face that part of ourselves.

In this regard, we need to guard against "blanket" confessions. Here is what a "blanket" confessor does: At the end of the day he or she says something like, "If I offended anyone, or if I was insensitive to anyone, or if I did not live up to my potential today, forgive me, Lord." In other words, "blanket" confessors never get specific. They never fully disclose the exact nature of the wrongdoing, and as a result, they never tap into God's forgiveness. To experience God's forgiveness, full disclosure is required.

For the next week try this. Every morning or evening go over the past twenty-four hours and get very specific with your offenses. In fact, take out a sheet of paper and write them down. It is amazing what seeing your wrongdoings in print will do for you. For example, you might write, "Yesterday I chose to wound my spouse with my words. I was cruel, insensitive, and sinful." Or you might write, "Last night I told my son I would play ball with him, and I did not. I did not keep my word." Or you might write, "This morning I overslept, ran late, and took it out on my roommate. I was selfish and inconsiderate." Try doing that for a week and see what happens.

- STEP TWO: *Turn to God.*

After removing these barriers to forgiveness, we are ready for the next step: We need to ask God to do what we cannot do on our own. Face it. Forgiveness is a supernatural act. We may want to be more gracious, we may want to be more forgiving, but it is humanly impossible to pull it off. We do not have the internal resources to do it. We can never, on our own, forgive others as God has forgiven us. We may want to become a forgiving person. We may work hard at becoming this kind of person. We may strive for it, but it will not happen consistently apart from Christ.

Christ is the taproot, the fountain of forgiveness, the key to forgiving others. His words, "Apart from me you can do nothing" (John 15:5) convey our need for his example, his resources, his love.

The great Scottish preacher Robert Murray M'Cheyne once preached a sermon on Jesus' words, "I am the door, if any one enters by me, he or she will be saved" (John 10:9). After the message a man came up to M'Cheyne and said, "Listening to you preach about Jesus' being the door, I realized what my problem has been all these years. I have been trying to enter the wrong door! I have been trying to go through the saints door, and I just couldn't make it. You made it clear today that I need to go through the sinner's door."

To forgive as God has forgiven us, we need to go through the "sinner's door." We need to face the fact that we cannot pull this off on our own. We need to admit our need for a power and love that is greater than ours.

GROUP DISCUSSION AND SHARING

1. **Icebreaker** *(15-20 minutes)*
   - Share an incident from childhood when your parents forgave you or withheld forgiveness from you.

2. **Discussion** *(15-20 minutes)*
   Comment on the following statements from this chapter:
   - "God's vertical forgiveness seems to go ahead of, and make possible, horizontal forgiveness." (pg 108)

- "This is not a gospel of calculators but a gospel of grace. We are to be typified by a forgiving spirit, with forgiveness as a continual attitude in our lives." (pg 102)
- "The message of Jesus' story is that forgiveness is unconditional. Jesus' death and resurrection were not contingent upon our behavior; he did not wait for us to say, 'We're sorry; we really blew it.'" (pg 106)
- "Face it. Forgiveness is a supernatural act. We may want to be more gracious, we may want to be more forgiving, but it is humanly impossible to pull it off. We do not have the internal resources to do it. We can never, on our own, forgive others as God has forgiven us. We may want to become a forgiving person. We may work hard at becoming this kind of person. We may strive for it, but it will not happen consistently apart from Christ." (pg 111)

3. **Forgiveness, You, and the Group** (*15-20 minutes*)
   - Rank the following actions in terms of the "toughest" to forgive if someone in your small group were to behave this way. Assign the number "1" to the toughest, number "2" the next toughest, and so on. Share your top three with the group.
     ____ They are constantly late for the group.
     ____ They missed group because they'd rather watch TV.
     ____ They broke a confidence.
     ____ They did not do the study.
     ____ They said my ideas or opinions were off-base.
     ____ They interrupted me when I was talking.
     ____ They spilled coffee on my new couch.
     ____ They monopolize group time with incessant talking.
     ____ They always give advice.
     ____ They never seem interested in what I have to say.

   - Engage in an act of forgiveness. Have the leader read the following instructions.

"Get as comfortable as you can. After you are comfortable, close your eyes and picture the face of someone you need to forgive. It may be an ex-spouse, a co-worker, a former friend, someone in this group. The person's face may also be a surprise to you. Trust the picture that comes to you.

"Now, tighten your fists and recall the hurt, the bitter words, the wrong deed, the way this person has let you down. With your fist clenched, think how easy it would be to strike back at them. Be aware of the hurt and anger that still remains between you and that person.

"Next, picture Jesus on the cross. See his suffering. Then look in the crowd around him and see the person who hurt you. Hear Jesus' words, 'Forgive them, for they know not what they do.' Let those words apply to the person you need to forgive. Begin seeing this person as Jesus might—see their inadequacies, their fears, the things that contributed to their actions.

"Slowly, open your fists and give that person to Jesus. Maybe you can't forgive this person yet. Maybe all you can do is say, 'Jesus, I know you want me to forgive this person; help me.' Let this be a starting point.

"When you are ready, open your eyes and let's talk about this experience."

4.   **Sharing Prayer Concerns** *(15-20 minutes)*

5.   **Pray Together** *(5 minutes)*

CHAPTER NINE

DO NOT ENVY ONE ANOTHER

If we live by the Spirit, let us also be guided by the Spirit.
Let us not become conceited,
competing against one another,
envying one another.
Galatians 5:25-26

I parked my car in the church parking lot. A parking lot security guard inquired about my business at the church. Taking a box of bulletin inserts out of the trunk of my car, I stated, "I'm delivering these inserts to the church office. I will only be a minute." He pointed me in the direction of the church office. It was a long walk. It was a mega-church.

On the way, I passed the church's newly constructed "Family Life Center." The Center was huge and attractive. I read signs about their newly formed elementary school that met in the Center. I walked by a couple of the church's maintenance people. They looked different from the maintenance people in my church. They wore shirts that matched and had their names sewn over their pockets. I thought to myself, "I wish our maintenance staff looked that classy."

When I reached the receptionist's office, I said to her, "I'm here on behalf of the Presbytery. I'm delivering these bulletin inserts describing the ministry of the Presbytery. I hope you will use them in the months ahead to inform your people what our Presbytery is doing." I paused a moment and then said, "Should I leave them here with you or should I leave them with someone else." She responded, "I'll call our Communications Director. He'll be down in a minute to talk to you."

I thought to myself, "'Communications Director?' They have a 'Communications Director'? I wish we had the luxury of having a Communications Director." As I stood waiting in the lobby, I watched the overhead television monitor tell me of upcoming events and the day's schedule. I thought to myself, "I wish we had a monitor like that in our church." I read the sign listing the pastoral staff. Seven pastors! They had five more than we had. I wished we had seven pastors. That way, I could do less of the stuff I did not like to do and more of what I really enjoyed. I observed young mothers coming to pick up their children from the elementary day school. I thought, "I wish we had an elementary school." I watched a young, attractive-looking couple ask to see one of the pastors. I surmised they had come for pre-marital counseling. I thought to myself, "No wonder they want to be married here. This church has a beautiful sanctuary, much nicer than ours. I wish we had a sanctuary like that." After waiting ten minutes, I left. The Director of Communications must have been diverted. When I got home, I looked up the congregation's web page on the Internet and e-mailed the Communications Director, telling him about the bulletins I had left. He had designed their web site. It was spectacular. I wished our web site looked that good.

ENVY DEFINED

Envy. Shakespeare called it "the green sickness." Bacon admitted it "has no holidays." The author of Proverbs wrote that envy "rots the bones." St. Augustine said, "It tortures the soul." Petrarch said, "It is the great enemy of inner peace," and the Apostle James claimed that envy "leads to disorder and wickedness of every kind" (James 3:16).

If you struggle with it, you know the damage it can cause. You know envy's effects. It has been called the "if only" disease:

> If only I had a car like his . . .
> If only I had a job like hers . . .
> If only I had a marriage like that . . .
> If only I were thin like she is . . .
> If only I could write like he does . . .

Webster defines envy as the "painful or resentful awareness of an advantage enjoyed by another joined with a desire to possess the same advantage."[1] As such, it varies from jealousy, even though we often use the words interchangeably. Jealousy starts with full hands and fears losing what it already has. Jealousy wants to keep what it has. Envy, on the other hand, starts with empty hands and mourns for what it does not have. Envy wants to possess what someone else has. As Thomas Aquinas appropriately said, envy is "sorrow at another's good." Envy, however, does more than sorrow. Envy desires full hands. Dorothy Sayers wrote, "Envy begins by asking plausibly: 'Why should I not enjoy what others enjoy?' and ends by demanding: 'Why should others enjoy what I may not?'"[2] Of the two, envy is the worse, for God refers to himself/herself as jealous (Deuteronomy 5:9), but never as envious.

ENVY IN THE BIBLE

There are numerous examples of envy throughout the Scriptures. One vivid example is the story of Joseph, who was sold by envy into slavery by his brothers. It started with a gift—a coat given to him by his father. Even though the Hebrew wording is vague, the coat appeared to be the kind of coat more closely associated with the leisure class than the working class. In our day it might be more akin to a smoking jacket. One would not be expected to work in such a garment. It had long sleeves, not short sleeves. The rest of the sons had short-sleeve coats—working garments—something akin to bib overalls. The symbolism was clear. Daddy expected them to work hard, while Joseph took it easy. They became envious of Joseph's exalted position. They also grew angry. The author of Genesis writes, "When his brothers saw that their father loved him more than all his brothers, they hated him, and could not speak peaceably to him." Envy drove them to drastic action: When Daddy turned his back, they tossed Joseph into a pit and sold him into slavery.

Envy also drove David into exile (1 Samuel 19:8-17). King Saul had an inferiority complex. David, his military commander and son-in-law, had no such problems. David always saw himself as the fair-haired boy, which he was, and he could charm the birds out of trees. Because of that, it was not long until half of Israel was in love with him. Maidens sang, "Saul has killed his thousands and David his tens of thousands," and Saul wanted what David had. He hungered for respect, love, charisma. Unable to get it, he opted for Plan B. He decided to remove David from the scene. Thankfully, David's wife, Saul's daughter, helped David escape one night under the cover of darkness. David was saddened by the entire affair. He liked Saul and only wanted to get along, but Saul despised David and only wanted what David had. Saul died a tragic death trying to get it.

Envy also threw Daniel in the lion's den. The story goes,

It pleased Darius to set over the kingdom one hundred twenty satraps, stationed throughout the whole kingdom, and over them three presidents, including Daniel; to these the satraps gave account, so that the king might suffer no loss. Soon Daniel distinguished himself above all the other presidents and satraps because an excellent spirit was in him, and the king planned to appoint him over the whole kingdom. (Daniel 6:1-3)

Of course, instead of being pleased with Daniel's success, his rivals became envious. They looked for information to bring him down, but could find none. Knowing, however, how much Daniel enjoyed praying to Yahweh, the God of Israel, they drew upon King Darius' immense ego and sense of nationalism, and proposed an edict saying that for thirty days no one could say prayers except to the great King Darius. If anyone was caught praying to anyone else, he would become brunch for the lions. Darius signed the ordinance on the spot.

Daniel, aware of the edict, conducted business as usual. As he always had done, three times a day he opened his window toward Jerusalem and prayed to Yahweh (Daniel 6:10). Inevitably, the prayer police caught him in the act and sent him to the lions. However, when Daniel survived the night, King Darius took it as a sign from God of Daniel's favor and sent the prayer police to the lions in Daniel's place. Before they reached the bottom of the den, the lions devoured them. The story only goes to show how envy can eat you alive.

Envy also brought Christ to the cross. Matthew tells us that it was out of envy that the Jewish officials handed Jesus over to Pilate (Matthew 27:18). Jesus' popularity and power had turned the religious officials against him. If they could not have what Jesus had, they would try to take it from him. The empty tomb foiled their plan.

ENVY TODAY

Someone once said, "The only thing we learn from history is that we do not learn from history." That certainly seems to be the case. Instead of learning a valuable lesson from the stories of Joseph, David, Daniel, and Jesus, we repeat the sins of the past. Envy continues to raise its ugly head in families, churches, neighborhoods, schools, and places of employment.

I smile at the story of an elderly woman who decided to have her portrait painted. She told the artist, "Paint me with diamond earrings, a diamond necklace, emerald bracelets, a ruby broach, and a gold Rolex."

The artist replied, "But you know you are not wearing any of those things."

"I know," she said. "It's in case I should die before my husband. I'm sure he will remarry right away, and I want his new wife to go crazy looking for the jewelry!"

Just in case she died first, she wanted her successor to be envious of her!

Perhaps the saddest place of all to find envy is in the church. The Apostle Paul hoped it would not be a distinguishing mark among Christ's people. He counseled, "Let us not become conceited, competing against one another, *envying* one another" (Galatians 6:26). But envy we do. Pastors envy other pastors' successes. Church members envy other church members' spiritual gifts. They wish they could teach like Jane or organize like Phil or sing like Bob. They envy the attention some folk in the church get that they do not get. They ask questions such as, "How come the pastor takes them to lunch and not me?" and "How come Judy was asked to serve as an elder and I wasn't? I do as much as she does." and "How come Bill gets all the recognition while I sit in the background? I do as much work, if not more, than he." They ask, usually quietly and only to themselves, "What do they have that I do not have?" Nothing, they conclude, and the green bile of envy churns in their stomachs.

Oscar Wilde tells a wonderful story in this regard:

> The devil was once crossing the Libyan desert, and he came upon a spot where a number of small fiends were tormenting a holy hermit. The sainted man easily shook off their evil suggestions. The devil watched their failure, and then he stepped forward to give them a lesson. "What you do is too crude," he said. "Permit me for one moment." With that he whispered to the holy man, *"Your brother has just been made Bishop of Alexandria."* A scowl of malignant jealousy at once clouded the serene face of the hermit. "That," said the devil to his imps, "is the sort of thing which I should recommend."[3]

Even the best of us, including saints, are susceptible to the green monster.

In the Middle Ages church leaders identified envy as one of the Seven Deadly Sins. These church leaders urged people to rid themselves of these sins—sloth, lust, anger, pride, envy, gluttony, greed—for they contended that out of them came the evil in the world. Today, there is little doubt in the minds of those who observe human behavior closely that envy is a major cause of unhappiness. It destroys relationships, breeds self-contempt, and sows seeds of discontentment.

I still painfully recall how envy soured my relationship with a pastoral colleague. During my days as an associate pastor, I served with a wonderful man. Denn Denning was energetic, visionary, and a great communicator. He possessed all the things I wanted to possess. So envious was I of Denn that I secretly hoped he would fail in the pulpit. I secretly hoped that he would preach a few "snoozers." He seldom did. But, when he did fail in the pulpit or in relationships, I felt better. If I could not attain Denn's level, then maybe he could descend to mine.

Journalist and author Henrie Fairlie called this "The Revenge of Failure." He claimed that taking pleasure in a gifted person's demise is the disease of our time. If we cannot paint well or write well—or preach well—then we take great pleasure when others, who do these things well, fail. The gossip column and the grocery store tabloid have become the symbols of our envious age. They reduce people of virtue, talent, and achievement to individuals who are "just like us," or in some cases, worse than us. In fact, Fairlie asserts that we feel cheated by our newspapers and magazines if no one is leveled in the dust in them. We wait in ambush for the novel that fails, for the poet who commits suicide, for the financier who is a crook, for the politician who slips, for the priest who commits a sexual indiscretion. We lie in ambush for them all, so that we may gloat at their misfortune. Fairlie says, "It has long been noted that *schadenfruede*—joy at the suffering of another—is peculiarly a mark of our age."[4]

At the funeral of Princess Diana, her younger brother, Earl Spencer, burst forth with an undiluted cry of pain and anger against the media. As he eulogized his sister, he commented, "I don't think she ever understood why her genuinely good intentions were sneered at by the media, why there appeared to be a permanent quest on their behalf to bring her down." He said, "It is baffling. My own and only explanation is that genuine goodness is threatening to those at the opposite end of the moral spectrum."[5]

If we cannot have what "they" have, then we will find pleasure, sweet revenge, in their personal failures. If we cannot attain goodness on our own, envy looks to destroy the good in others. In the process, we succumb to backbiting, innuendo, accusations and, ultimately, envy destroys our relationships, breaking them apart at the seams.

Envy also diminishes our enjoyment of life. Recently, I took up golf. I have only been playing for a few months, and I constantly need to remember, "It's only a game." When I get frustrated that I can't shoot in the eighties or nineties like some of my golfing buddies, I think, "This is ridiculous. After all, here I am, outside with friends in a beautiful locale—luscious fairways, well-groomed greens, picturesque lake and bunkers—and I am not enjoying the experience." Because I want to shoot better, to play like my friends, I end up depriving myself of the joy of the game.

Jesus once told a story about a father with two boys. The younger boy was a free spirit and the older was a typical firstborn—dependable and responsible. After the younger brother squandered his fortune in loose-living, he came back home a broken and contrite man. The father took him back, threw a big barbecue for him, and invited all the neighbors, but the elder brother was a no-show. His problem? The older brother could not enjoy the celebration because he envied the attention lavished on his younger sibling. He had been invited to the party, but envy kept him from it. He failed to appreciate all his father had given him through the years.

Envy not only destroys relationships and diminishes our enjoyment of life, but it can also breed self-contempt. While in college I remember reading *The Autobiography of Malcolm X*. Malcolm X, murdered in the 1960s in Harlem, told how his envy of white people almost ruined him psychologically. He purchased skin creams to lighten his skin. He bought hair straighteners to make his hair more like that of white people. His envy of what white people had, and he did not, turned him to hating whites for a time. He joined, and eventually became a leader of, the Black Muslims, which preached racial superiority of blacks. Later, after a dramatic conversion experience to Islam, he softened his attitudes and worked for racial equality. He was able to turn around the self-contempt bred by envy to the point where he helped coin the phrase "Black is Beautiful."

All of us are potential "self-contempt" casualties. Women who envy the slim figures of models may despise their own bodies. Men who envy athletic prowess of sports stars may not recognize their own abilities in other areas. Students who envy more popular classmates may discount their own qualities.

GETTING A HANDLE ON ENVY

Envy . . . where is it lurking in your life? Here are some questions to help you gauge whether the needle on your "envy tank" points to full or empty:

- How easy is it to celebrate someone else's success or good fortune?
- Do you find yourself just as excited for someone else as you would be for yourself when they receive a promotion or a new car or an award at school or some special recognition? Or are you more likely to feel cheated and resentful?
- Do you tend to discount someone else's success by saying things such as, "He has connections; that's why he got the job," or "Sure, our house could look like that if we could afford a housekeeper."

Just in case envy may be getting the best of you, here are some steps to help in getting a handle on envy.

- <u>STEP ONE</u>: *Give thanks for what you already possess.*

In his book *The Seven Deadly Sins*, Tony Campolo gives a wonderful example of being appreciative:

> Giving thanks is a wonderful therapy for envy. My wife uses this remedy with great success and I attribute her optimism and contentment to her ability to see the positive aspects of her circumstances, whatever they may be. If we miss an airplane and have to wait two hours for the next one, she looks upon the two-hour wait as a gift from God so that the two of us can have this uninterrupted time to visit with each other. If I go out in the morning and find that my car battery is dead, she tells me how lucky I am that I did not have this trouble when I was out on some deserted highway.

If my coat gets ripped, she welcomes the opportunity to buy a new one . . .

Now I ask you, how can I not love a woman like that?

When I asked her if she ever felt the grass was greener on the other side of the fence, she answered, "If you think that the grass is greener on the other side of the fence, it is probably because you are not properly caring for the grass on your own side." If each of us would care for and appreciate the possibilities in what we have, we would cease to envy what others have.[6]

Focusing on what we have rather than what we do not will go a long way toward taming the green monster.

  • STEP TWO: *Learn the value of things.*
James Peterson caused quite a stir on May 6, 1991. That was the day his book *The Day America Told the Truth: What People Really Believe About Everything That Really Matters* hit the bookshelves. He posed a question that really caught my eye: "What are you honestly willing to do for ten million dollars?" Twenty-five percent of Americans would abandon their family. Twenty-three percent would become a prostitute for a week. Sixteen percent would renounce their citizenship. Seven percent would kill a stranger. Four percent would have a sex-change operation.[7] But ten million dollars is not the answer. Just ask Howard Hughes.

It was reported that all Hughes wanted was more. He wanted more money, so he parlayed inherited wealth into a billion-dollar pile of assets. He wanted more fame, so he broke into Hollywood and became a film maker. He wanted more sensual pleasures, so he paid handsome sums to indulge every urge. He wanted more thrills, so he designed and built the fastest aircraft in the world. He wanted more power, so he dealt political favors to the highest government officials in the land. He was absolutely convinced that more would bring him true satisfaction. Unfortunately, Hughes never got enough. He concluded his life emaciated, colorless, with fingernails shaped in grotesque, inches-long corkscrews. He died pursuing the myth of more.

Howard Hughes had not learned the true value of things. He died after drinking cup after cup of sand. Before you shake your head and ask, "How could someone be so stupid," consider this: "Has your most recent acquisition quenched the thirst in your soul?"

- STEP THREE: *Know your calling.*

Martin Luther, that giant of the Protestant Reformation, confessed, "Next to faith, this is the greatest art: to be content with the calling in which God has placed you." This raises a few questions to ponder:

- How content are you with your gifts and talents?
- Is it okay to have certain gifts and not others?
- How well do you know and accept your limits?

I think of Charles Cerling, Jr., who enjoys recreational volleyball even though he is only five feet, seven inches tall. Because of that, he does not spike the ball very often in his volleyball league. Yet, he frequently makes a set from backcourt that yields a smashing, point-winning spike. The spiker gets the praise and much of the glory, but Charles is a vital part of that team. Is it okay that you might be the setter and not the spiker?

I read about a guy I would like to meet. His name is Steve Harris, and he is the pastor of a small, country church. In America, we sometimes think pastors are successful only if they have a large church. Steve, though, knows his calling: "I'm not sure I would be able to be a pastor of a 'superchurch.' I don't have the preaching and organizational gifts for that. But some people in my church on the side of Highway 55 are struggling with their marriages. One woman's husband is dying with cancer. A girl who just graduated from high school is wondering what she will do with the rest of her life. Those are significant issues. They don't get much bigger. And it is in those places, as a simple country pastor, that I shine."

As Oswald Chambers has said, "God puts his saints where they will glorify him, and we are no judges at all of where that is."

When we can be comfortable with where we are, we will have gotten a handle on envy.

GROUP DISCUSSION AND SHARING

1. **Icebreaker** *(15-20 minutes)*
    - Share a time in the past when you were "green with envy."

2. **Discussion** *(15-20 minutes)*
    Discuss the following quotes from this chapter:

    - "Jealousy starts with full hands and fears losing what it already has. Jealousy wants to keep what it has. Envy, on the other hand, starts with empty hands and mourns for what it does not have. Envy wants to possess what someone else has. Of the two, envy is the worse, for God refers to himself/herself as jealous (Deut. 5:9), but never as envious." (pg. 115-116)

    - "Today, there is little doubt in the minds of those who observe human behavior closely that envy is a major cause of unhappiness. It destroys relationships, breeds self-contempt, and sows seeds of discontentment." (pg. 119)

    - "How easy is it to celebrate someone else's success or good fortune? Do you find yourself just as excited for someone else as you would be for yourself when they receive a promotion or a new car or an award at school or some special recognition? Or are you more likely to feel cheated and resentful?" (pg. 121)

3. **Personal Inventory** *(15-30 minutes)*
    - Step one in getting a handle on envy is giving thanks for what you already possess. Take five to ten minutes to turn your attention from others' achievements and blessings to your own. Count them one by one. Make a list of what God has done for you. After the list is complete, take time in the group to share one of them. When everyone in the group has had a chance to speak, offer two minutes of silent prayer, thanking God for giving so much.

    - Another step in getting a handle on envy involves knowing your calling. What do you especially like about what God has currently called you to be doing? Share at least three of these with the members of your small group.

4. **Sharing Prayer Concerns** *(10-15 minutes)*

5. **Prayer** *(5 minutes)*

CHAPTER TEN

BE HOSPITABLE TO ONE ANOTHER

Be hospitable to one another without complaining.
1 Peter 4:9

"You must hurry," friends cried to the teacher as he rushed home from the fields. "The banquet at the home of Halil has already begun. You are late."

"They are right," the teacher thought. "If I take time to change clothes, I could miss the entire dinner." Instead of returning to his home, he proceeded in his work clothes to the home of Halil, the rich man.

When he arrived, the servants at the door refused to allow him to enter because he was not dressed properly. Though he protested, the servants stood firm.

Finally, the teacher walked to the home of a friend who lived nearby. He borrowed a nice coat and quickly returned to the party. He was immediately welcomed and was seated at the banquet table.

When dinner was served, the teacher began to put the food on his coat. He smeared his jacket with vegetables and poured the appetizer in his pocket. All the time he said loudly, "Eat, dear dinner jacket. I hope you enjoy the meal."

All the guests focused their attention on the teacher's strange behavior. Finally, Halil asked, "Why are you telling your jacket to enjoy the meal?"

"When I arrived in my work clothes," the teacher explained, "I was refused entrance. It was only when I was accompanied by this fine coat that I was allowed to sit at the table. Naturally I assume it was the jacket, not me, that was invited to your banquet."[1]

Webster defines hospitality as "offering a pleasant or sustaining environment."[2] In other words, hospitality makes room for people. Hospitality opens doors to rich and poor, young and old, seedy and saintly. Hospitality offers generous and cordial space to others. The Bible describes hospitality in two ways: as a spiritual gift and as a command. Let's take a look at both.

HOSPITALITY AS A SPIRITUAL GIFT

Some do not include hospitality in the list of "spiritual gifts" because most references to it appear to cover a general standard of behavior expected of all of God's people, not just a special few. In that regard, the gift of hospitality is like the gift of giving. Even though we are all to "give generously," some in our midst do it more naturally and easily. They welcome the opportunity to give away twenty, thirty, fifty percent of their income. These people possess the gift of giving. The same is true for the gift of hospitality. Though we are all called to practice hospitality, some possess an uncanny ability to provide a warm, welcoming space for strangers.

For example, I lead small group seminars throughout the United States. I have been to California, Alaska, Nebraska, Texas, Georgia, Maine, Pennsylvania—just about every state in the Union—talking about the nuts-and-bolts of small group life. (I am still hoping, however, to receive a speaking engagement in Hawaii. There must be someone in that island paradise who could use some valuable small group counsel!) On my way to a small group seminar, I often say a little prayer just prior to boarding the airplane: "Please let there be an empty seat next to me on this flight, but if that's not possible, please let me sit next to someone who doesn't like to talk." If that fails, and I end up with the poster person for Mr/Ms Extrovert in the seat next to me, I bury my head in a book and give short answers to their questions. In other words, I do not offer a cordial or pleasant space. I obviously do not possess the gift of hospitality. As an introvert, I would rather close doors than open them. I would just as soon be left alone when I travel.

Barb Ludy is just the opposite. I met Barb in Omaha, Nebraska, when we were in a small group together. Unlike me, Barb would pray for people to sit next to her whenever she traveled—preferably someone who wanted to talk. When she would return to our small group, she would share amazing accounts of people she had met and conversations that had an impact on her and others. Barb made it easy to be in her presence. She loves people. People love her. She definitely has the gift of hospitality.

The New Testament word for hospitality is *philoxenos,* which means "love or fondness of strangers," and it comes from two Greek words: *philos,* meaning friendliness, and *xenos,* meaning stranger, alien or outsider. Few, however, possess this "love or fondness for strangers," probably because it is not all that natural. Primitive humanity's basic unit was the family. Anyone outside the family posed a threat, a challenge. To survive, one regarded the stranger with great suspicion. Much of that still carries over into the world in which we live. We say such things as "blood is thicker than water," and we often distrust the stranger in our midst. We bond together in clubs, fraternities, tribes, cults, religions, and anyone who does not belong to our group is an "outsider."

But the message of Christ instructs us to do the opposite, to welcome the stranger. In fact, one of the unique aspects of the Christian faith is the "great commission" to reach out and evangelize the stranger, the outsider. Not only that, we are to act as Good Samaritans to strangers in need.

Even though this applies to all of us, there are those certain individuals who have a special grace for reaching out and receiving strangers in their homes, churches, and neighborhoods. These people delight in meeting new persons and quickly respond to the special needs of strangers for lodging, food, and companionship.

C. Peter Wagner defines this gift of hospitality as "that special ability that God gives to certain members of the Body of Christ to provide an open house and warm welcome for those in need of food and lodging."[3] According to Wagner, people with this gift have a supernatural ability of opening their homes to others. In fact, people with the gift of hospitality are more comfortable with guests in their home than they are alone. They can hardly wait for company to arrive! They love having people in their homes, making them feel welcomed and cared for. People without the gift, however, can hardly wait for company to leave! If you have ever caught yourself saying, "Fish and company begin to smell after three days," you most likely do not possess the gift of hospitality.

In describing this gift Wagner recommends one resource and one caution. The resource is Karen Mains' book *Open Heart, Open Home.*[4] Karen, who possesses the gift of hospitality, claims "hospitality over pride" as her motto. That is to say, she has no need for things to be "straightened up" before she is comfortable having company in her home. The newspapers do not need to be put away. Dirty dishes do not need to be placed in the dishwasher. The carpet does not need to be vacuumed. She might feel better if her house were cleaner, but what is most important to her is an open door, not an immaculate home. When things are not "spic and span" around her home, she would much rather have her pride as a housekeeper take a hit than turn anyone away from her door.

Bruce Bugbee, in his spiritual gifts course developed at Willow Creek Church outside Chicago, broadens the definition of "hospitality" to include fellowship as well as food and lodging.[5] That is to say, hospitality means more than having folk over for dinner or always having one's guestroom full. According to Bugbee, hospitality also invites people into one's presence, not just into one's home. One can express this gift on an airplane, as does Barb Ludy, or in a church, or in a checkout line at a grocery store. Wherever we go, according to Bugbee, we can invite people into our "personal space" and make them feel welcomed and important.

Wagner, however, raises a caution flag when it comes to the gift of hospitality. As is the case with any spiritual gift, we can fall into the trap of what he calls "gift projection," where we expect everyone to do, through human effort, what we have been particularly gifted to do through the Spirit. Each of us is given a gift, but not necessarily the same gifts. If we do not possess the gift of hospitality, if our home is more our castle than a "way station for others," we are not to beat ourselves over the head. We do, however, have to work at it, because hospitality is not only a spiritual gift but is also a biblical command.

HOSPITALITY AS A COMMAND

Some people have the gift of faith, yet we are all called to exercise our faith. Some people have the gift of giving, yet all of us are called to give. Just so, some people have the gift of hospitality, yet we are all called to practice it. The Apostle Peter writes, "Be hospitable to one another without complaining."

The biblical world depended upon everyone being hospitable. The story of Sodom and Gomorrah (Genesis 19:1-11) comes to mind. Lot, Abraham's nephew, had settled in raunchy Sodom. God was about to destroy the city, but as a favor to Abraham, God agreed to save Lot from the impending destruction. God sent two angels to retrieve Lot. When they arrived at the city gates, Lot did not know they were angels, and he had no idea why they had come. Yet he did what any good person of that day would do—he offered his home for lodging. At first, the two strangers declined, but Lot prevailed upon them, and he took them into his home and prepared a feast for them.

Then, tensions rose. The men of Sodom surrounded the house and demanded that Lot send out his two guests so that they might have sex with them. Lot offered an alternative. To appease the crowd, Lot offered his two virgin daughters instead of his house guests. He said, "Look, I have two daughters who have not known a man; let me bring them out to you and do to them as you please; only do nothing to these men, for they have come under the shelter of my roof" (Genesis 19:8).

In our day and time, such a plan sounds despicable. Why would anyone offer his daughters "to do with them as they pleased?" Was this just another sign of a patriarchal society where men were valued and women were viewed as property? Was this an example of the sexism that seems to run rampant in biblical stories? Not entirely. The main concern was honoring the bonds of hospitality. Lot had taken the two strangers under his roof, and as a host, it was his job to protect his guests, no matter the cost—even if it meant the lives of his daughters or his own life.

This practice of hospitality stemmed from nomadic life, where public inns were a rarity. People never knew when they would be dependent on others. As a result, guests were treated with respect and honor and were provided with food supplies for their animals, water for their feet, lodging, and a sumptuous feast. Guests enjoyed protection for three days and thirty-six hours after eating with the host.[6] Hospitality was to the Bedouin what almsgiving was to the later Jews—an expression of righteousness. A traveler entering a city would come to the city gates, and there, unless a breach of etiquette occurred, someone, like Lot, would invite the traveler to his home and offer the customary graces. To break the bond of hospitality was the worst thing a host could do.

In the New Testament Jesus, too, was dependent on people practicing hospitality. When he was in Jerusalem, he stayed in the home of Martha, Mary, and Lazarus in nearby Bethany. The practice of hospitality helps to explain how Jesus could so easily have said to the diminutive tax collector, "Zacchaeus, hurry and come down; for I must stay at your house today" (Luke 19:5). Hospitality was simply expected in Jesus' day. The practice of hospitality also accounts, to a considerable degree, for the extensive journeys of the early Christian missionaries. In their travels they would seek out other Christians with whom to stay. For example, Lydia said to Paul, "If you have judged me to be faithful to the Lord, come and stay at my home" (Acts 16:15). And when Apollos prepared to take the message into Achaia, "the believers encouraged him and wrote to the disciples to welcome him" (Acts 18:27). It is no surprise that the Apostle Peter reminded people to practice hospitality without complaint.

The words "without complaint," however, suggest that some folk in Peter's churches were resisting the practice of hospitality. Maybe they had begun to complain and begrudge the duty to provide room and lodging for Christian travelers. Maybe, since the church had no buildings at that time, those with bigger houses were getting tired of opening up their homes for meetings. Certainly some welcomed the opportunity to offer their homes for corporate worship and fellow-ship—people such as Aquila and Priscilla (Romans 16:5; 1 Corinthians 16:19) and Philemon (Philemon 2). In fact, without the Aquilas and Priscillas and Philemons, the church could not have met for worship at all. But perhaps, for others, the burden was too much.

Who knows what was actually behind Peter's command to "be hospitable without complaining." Whether the problem was begrudging a constant stream of out-of-town house guests, or begrudging having to put up with a crowd in their living room on Sunday morning, it was a great concern to Peter. And he was not alone. Again and again the duty of hospitality was pressed upon the saints. The Apostle Paul recommended it to all believers (Romans 12:13). The author of Hebrews reminded Christians that, by entertaining strangers, they just might be entertaining angels unawares (Hebrews 13.:2). Jesus' words, especially, haunt us: "I was a stranger and you welcomed me" (Matthew 25:35). Though we may not all be gifted in hospitality, there is no question that we are to practice it wherever we are—and without complaint. Hospitality is not just a gift. It is a biblical command.

HOSPITALITY IN CHURCHES

A number of years ago we invited some consultants into our congregation. We had reached a plateau where worship attendance and church membership had hovered at the same level for three years, and we wanted to see what was inhibiting our growth. The consultants came on a Friday night. They took me and my wife to dinner, and we talked informally about the congregation. On Saturday they met with the church officers and toured the church building. On Saturday night the consultants met with a cross-section of the congregation, about sixty people. On Sunday morning, they attended worship and met with us afterward for a "de-briefing" lunch in the church basement.

Many things stand out about that closing lunch, but nothing more vividly than the fact that we had failed "the visitors test." As a congregation, we had thought we were warm and friendly. We were not.

The consultants had assigned points to how many times someone spoke, smiled, or nodded at them. I do not remember the exact point system, but it went something like this: 1 point for a nod; 3 points for a smile; 5 points if they were welcomed at the door by greeters; 5 points if an usher gave them a bulletin and escorted them to a seat; 10 points if there was a greeting time during the service; 20 points if someone who was not an usher or greeter talked to them; 30 points if that person took them to meet a church staff member; 40 points if someone asked them to join them in the fellowship hall for coffee; and 100 points if they were invited to brunch or lunch after worship. We flunked the test. Other than greeters and ushers, who were *supposed* to talk to strangers, no one else had spoken to the consultants.

Church sociologist Herb Miller has a chapter in one of his books entitled "Set Your Thermostat on Friendly." He begins with these words:

> The pastor was astonished at his welcome. He had just arrived at an ancient Coptic monastery out in the desert, nearly a day's journey from Cairo, Egypt. The monks treated him as if he were the one important guest they had been awaiting since the place was established in the twelfth century. They served a fine meal, showed him to a comfortable room, and brought him a bouquet of flowers. He was then greeted by the abbot of the monastery, Father Jeremiah.
>
> "Wow!" said the pastor. "You sure know how to treat visitors."
>
> Father Jeremiah replied, "We always treat guests as if they were angels, just to be safe."[7]

In this high-tech age, people long for a high-touch church. As Warren J. Hartman, research director for The United Methodist

Church, says, "When both unchurched and churched people are asked what they look for in a church . . . all of them agree about one factor—the climate of the congregation. They are looking for a church in which they feel at home, where people are friendly, and where there is warmth and a comfortable atmosphere."[8]

I think of Wendy Snow-Lewis, a member of our congregation who helps us pass "the visitors test." After worship, she invites everyone she can to join her and her husband for lunch. Wendy calls her group "Bunch for Lunch," and every Sunday four to twenty people, however many she can talk into going, join her and her husband at a local restaurant. The restaurant changes week to week, but not Wendy. Every visitor she meets at worship, she invites to lunch that day!

In a world where more and more people feel like a number, it is all the more important that churches practice the command of hospitality by welcoming strangers, making them feel at home, calling them by name—and inviting them to lunch!

HOSPITALITY IN SMALL GROUPS

Small groups present a particular problem when it comes to church hospitality. People who are not in a group often view small groups as cliquish and inhospitable, and, all too often, they have just cause for their negative perception. They may have tried to join a small group only to be told, "We do not have room in our group for anyone else." Anyone considering starting small groups in his or her congregation needs to ask, "How can we keep small groups from becoming cliquish in our church?"

In response to that question, I offer two recommendations. First, create an "open chair" in the group. That is, the group stays open to adding new people to the group until the group reaches a certain size. Then when the group reaches that size, say twelve, the group commits to giving birth to another group by sending two or three from the group to form another group. Both groups, the parent group and the "newborn" group, repeat the process keeping an open chair available to new people who might want to join the group.

This is how it worked in one of my small groups: We began with seven and decided that twelve would be an optimum size. We put an empty chair in our circle, and each week we prayed about someone to fill that chair. Eventually, people did fill the chair and we grew to twelve. When we reached that point, we sent two people from our group to give birth to another group. After they left, we had room for two new people to join our group and the newborn group had room for ten more people.

Of course, care must be taken when inviting people into that open chair. The open chair is not intended for guests who have no intention of joining the group. Rather, the chair is open to anyone who is serious about becoming a member of the group. Also, the group needs to decide who they will invite into the group. For example, if Frank asked me if he might join our group, I would tell him, "Frank, let me ask the group, but I think it would be fine." Then I would take Frank's name to the group the next week and tell them of his interest and his desire to be in our group. The group would then extend Frank an invitation to be in the group with the following stipulation: "Frank, we would love you to be in the group, but we want you to commit to four meetings before you decide to stay in the group or leave the group. We ask this because it takes awhile to get to know one another, and some days the group functions better than other days, so we want you to give us a chance before you decide whether you are in or out. We think four sessions should give you a good sense of the group."

Bringing names to the group for approval also helps the group manage the growth of the group. By knowing how many people are joining, and when they will be joining, the group can better integrate newcomers into the group. From a practical standpoint, if invitations were not cleared in advance, a group could conceivably have five or six newcomers show up at its next meeting! If the group already had ten members, that would put the group at sixteen, well over the optimum size for a small group. The group would then be forced to make some instant decisions about dividing and giving birth to another group. Clearing invitations in advance avoids such a crisis.

The second recommendation is for small groups to view larger congregation gatherings as "extended family." Even though small groups may have created a sense of support and belonging within the group, that does not necessarily overflow into the life of the congregation. In fact, just the opposite frequently happens. Instead of helping others in the church feel like they also belong, small group members tend to huddle together at church functions. They tend to make a beeline for one another after worship. They tend to talk to one another in fellowship hall. They tend to converge together at church socials and overlook those not in their group. As a result, people in the church see "small groupers" as standoffish, uninterested in them. To combat this,

I recommend the "two-minute drill." That is, when your group is at worship or at a potluck supper, make it a practice to speak to someone *outside* the group for two minutes before speaking to someone in the group. A friend of mine puts it this way: "When in the group, focus on one another. When outside the group, focus on God's extended family."

In fact, some small groups have adopted "hospitality" as their group's ministry. They study the ministry of hospitality in Scripture and through materials gathered from various resources. They view Sunday morning as a public event where strangers are expected and welcomed. Instead of signing up as "formal" greeters or ushers or follow-up callers, they strategically place themselves throughout the sanctuary looking for newcomers. They also stand in the church narthex or fellowship hall keeping an eye out for people standing alone. When they spot such a person or such a family, they go over to them, strike up a conversation, and work toward making them feel welcome.

In other words, they take seriously the words of the Apostle Peter: "Be hospitable to one another without complaining."

GROUP DISCUSSION AND SHARING QUESTIONS

1. **Icebreaker** (20-30 *minutes*)
    Complete the following:
    *   "When it comes to projecting warmth and hospitality to others I am . . . "
        ___ Below freezing
        ___ A little nippy
        ___ A gentle breeze
        ___ Warm and cozy
        ___ Hot and humid

    *   "When I first visited our church/community of faith, I found it to be . . ."
        ___ Below freezing
        ___ A little nippy
        ___ A gentle breeze
        ___ Warm and cozy
        ___ Hot and humid

- "Something our group could do to practice hospitality is . . ."

2. **Discussion** *(15-20 minutes)*
Complete this sentence:
    - "Something from this chapter that struck me as insightful or important was . . ."

3. **Sharing Prayer Concerns** *(20-25 minutes)*

4. **Prayer** *(5-10 minutes)*

CHAPTER ELEVEN

HONOR ONE ANOTHER

Love one another with mutual affection;
outdo one another in showing honor.
Romans 12:10

"What an *honor!*"

"She graduated with *honors.*"

"Jeff popped the question. Would you be my Maid of *Honor?*"

"Do you promise to tell the truth, the whole truth, and nothing but the truth, so help you God?" . . . "Yes, your *Honor.*"

"He received an *honorable* mention."

"*Honor* your father and your mother" (Exodus 20:12).

"I promise to do it—Scout's *Honor!*"

"He was *honorably* discharged from military service in October of 1995."

"Will you have this woman as your wife and will you pledge yourself to her in all love and *honor* . . . to live with her and cherish her according to the ordinance of God in the holy bond of marriage?"

"She has a hearing before the *Honor* Board tomorrow morning."

"We need to *honor* our previous commitment."

"I made the *honor* roll this semester."

"I give the rest of my allotted time to the *honorable* senator from the great state of Wisconsin."

C learly we use the word "honor," and its derivatives, in a number of ways. We use it to show merited respect. We use it to address someone in high office. We use it during ceremonial rites or observances. We use it to protect someone's reputation. We use it to describe a person of integrity. We use it to pay a compliment.

When Jesus used the word "honor," he used it in reference to God (John 8:49) and in reference to himself, claiming the same honor as paid to God (John 5:23). Furthermore, he applied force to the commandment to honor one's parents by criticizing some adult children for failing to provide financial support for their needy parents (Mark 7:10).

Jesus' followers employed the word honor as well. Peter summoned husbands to honor their wives out of loving regard (1 Peter 3:7), and he instructed all believers to honor all people, specifically rulers (1 Peter 2:17). Paul followed suit, instructing us to outdo one another in showing honor (Romans 12:10).

The word honor means "to value," "to respect," or "to give worth." That is what a little church in England failed to do. One Sunday while on vacation, John Henry Jowett, the great English preacher, visited a quiet village chapel and took his seat almost unnoticed in the congregation. As time approached for the beginning of the service, the visiting preacher had not arrived. The deacons asked if anyone would be willing to give the morning message. Jowett, a stranger to the congregation, volunteered.

Jowett preached a sermon he had recently preached in his own church, Carr's Lane, one of the great churches in England. The congregation did not respond well to the sermon, but the deacons thanked him for helping them out in a pinch. During the week the local newspaper announced that Jowett of Birmingham was enjoying his holiday there. When the deacons realized who he was, they approached him to preach again on Wednesday night. Jowett was surprised by the invitation.

"I preached for you Sunday," he said.

"Yes," the deacons replied, "but we did not know then that you were John Henry Jowett of Carr's Lane!"

Their lack of respect kept them from hearing the good news Jowett had already preached.

Outdoing one another in showing honor goes a long way toward building healthy relationships. Francine Klagsbrun wrote a book entitled *Married People: Staying Together in the Age of Divorce* in which she interviewed eighty-seven couples who had been married fifteen years or longer. As she searched for a common denominator for why they stayed together, she found one common thread: respect.[1] In healthy marriages, couples honor one another. In healthy groups, members do the same. Of course, someone might ask, how does a small group go about doing such a thing? How does a small group outdo one another in showing honor? In response to that question, consider the following.

SHOWING HONOR IN SMALL GROUPS

- *FIRST, a small group honors one another by beginning and ending on time.*

My wife and I have an ongoing battle over time. My idea of being on time is to be five minutes early. When getting somewhere, I allow extra time for traffic jams, accidents, or taking a wrong turn. I hate being late. I think it springs from my parents' divorce. When I was a young boy, I recall many a Friday evening when my mother would not allow my father to take me to his apartment for the weekend. His crime? He was late picking me up. My father promised my mother he would be there by 6:00 P.M. But if he did not arrive by the appointed hour, my mother would see that as a sign of disrespect. If he called and said he would be late, that was okay. We could still spend the weekend together, but to arrive late without a call was a different matter.

As a result, at an early age I learned that some people interpret being late as a sign of disrespect. As a little boy, I vowed to be where I was supposed to be, on time.

My wife, Trudy, on the other hand, approaches time more elastically. If she arrives within five minutes of the appointed hour, she considers herself "on time." Not only that, she expects the best to happen when traveling. She expects green lights and no traffic. In fact, that is her main problem. It is not that she is a poor time manager. It is just that she thinks she can accomplish more in a period of time than is usually possible. She attempts to do "one more thing" before she leaves, which results in her arriving "in the nick of time" or a few minutes late. As a result, she runs on what I call "Trudy time." When she says she will be home in five minutes, I allow ten. When she says, "I'll be there in half an hour," I allow forty-five minutes.

Most of the time I view her being "a little late" as an endearing personality trait, but not always. Every now and then I resent it. I say to myself, "If she really loved me, she would be on time. If she respected me, she would not make me wait."

Something similar can take place in a small group. For some group members, being on time is not a big deal. For others it is a major issue, especially if certain individuals are chronically late. When people consistently arrive past the appointed hour, some group members may see this as a sign of disrespect. To respect those for whom time is important, group members who honor one another will strive to arrive on time.

They will also strive to end the group on time. When we had small children, it drove Trudy and me nuts when our small group went past the stated ending time. Our group was supposed to meet from 7:30 P.M. to 10:00 P.M. Invariably, the group would go past 10:00 o'clock. When the clock struck 10:00, the group leader would say, "I know we are supposed to end now, but would you mind going a few minutes past the hour so we will have time to pray for one another?" Trudy and I regularly had to say no because we had a baby-sitter who needed to be home by 10:30 on school nights. Since we were the only ones in the group with small children, we felt as if we were constantly being put on the spot. If the group leader had done a better job of honoring the time, we would not have been placed in such an awkward position. Eventually the group realized it needed to end, as well as start, on time, but not without some frustration.

For many people the ending time is important. Some have to get up early the next morning for work. Some are morning people rather than night people, and they begin wearing down as the evening progresses. Some hate it when the group regularly goes past the appointed hour as a result of poor planning or the lack of group discipline. Therefore, groups who outdo one another in showing honor begin and end on time.

● *SECOND, a small group shows honor by conducting the meeting with whoever is present.*

I once had lunch with an exasperated couple. They had "had it" with their small group, so much so that they were considering leaving. What had gotten under their skin was the fact that their small group kept postponing the study until the following week. This had happened four weeks in a row. The couple said, "Each week we go to the group intending to do the study, but then we don't do it because some people are missing. But what about us? We have done our homework. We have come prepared. Why do we have to wait to do the study just because some people are absent? We want to be in a group that does a study. Half the time we never do one because people are absent. Do you know of a group we can join that regularly does a study?"

There is an old story about the preacher who held worship after a twelve-inch snow storm. Instead of the normal fifty people in church, only one man, a determined farmer, attended that day. The pastor looked at the man and thought about canceling the service. Then he thought better of the idea. He said to himself, "Well, if Farmer Brown made the effort to get here this morning, I will conduct the worship service just as if the normal crowd were present."

So the pastor did. He made sure they sang all three hymns. He led Farmer Brown in the prayer of confession, the prayer of thanksgiving, and the pastoral prayer. They recited the Apostles' Creed and sang the Gloria Patri, and the pastor preached his normal twenty-minute sermon. After the service the pastor asked Farmer Brown, "What did you think of the service today?"

The farmer said, "Fine, but when I only have one cow to feed, I don't give her the whole bale!"

Small groups, however, function best when the people present, no matter how few, get "the whole bale." To skip studies, to cut meetings short because a handful of people are absent, does a disservice to those who have made the time to attend the group. Those who miss ought to bear the consequences of their absence, not the ones who made the effort to come. Healthy groups honor the people present. They do not wait for everyone to arrive before they begin the group. Latecomers are greeted with something like, "Welcome . . . We were just doing . . ." and the group continues, avoiding long explanations or starting again. Those present, then, benefit from not having to cut things short or out of the meeting.

- *THIRD, groups honor one another by doing the assigned homework.*

Imagine a group of five men. They meet in a restaurant every Friday for lunch where they have a back room reserved just for them. Their homework assignment for the next session is to come prepared to answer four questions:

"Who am I?"
"What am I here for?"
"What is my purpose?"
"Where am I going when I die?"

The next week arrives, and only one of the five guys has done the assignment. The others forgot. They decide to give each other another week to complete the assignment, but how do you think the guy who came prepared thought and felt? What do they do if some forget to do the assignment the next week? Do they postpone the discussion again?

Or imagine being in a mixed group—male and female, couples and singles. The group is studying a chapter a week in Catherine Marshall's book *The Helper*. A third of the group, however, arrives not having read the chapter. How does that affect the discussion? Is the discussion richer or poorer for some not having completed the assignment? How do those who did the homework think and feel about those who did not read the chapter, especially if these individuals jump into the discussion with both feet?

Healthy groups honor commitments. They do what they say they will do, when they say they will do it. Not doing group "homework," however, plagues many groups, so much so that some groups have gone to one of two extremes. One extreme is to adopt a rule that if you do not do the assigned reading, you may not participate in the group discussion.

The other extreme is to eliminate "homework." When a majority of people are not completing the assignment, some groups decide to do studies that require no homework. These groups live off such "prompts" as the margin questions in *The Serendipity Bible* or they read a chapter of a book out loud, as a group. The leader then peppers the group with questions on what they have just read. However, studies that require no preparation are scarce. Groups that commit to doing some advanced reading generally have more satisfying studies and have more resources available to them.

  • *FOURTH, groups honor one another by listening attentively.*

Stephen Covey relates the following experience.

At one time, I was training two hundred MBA students at an eastern university, and many faculty and invited guests were there as well. We took the toughest, most sensitive, most vulnerable issue they could come up with—abortion. We had a pro-life person and a pro-choice person who both felt really deeply about their positions come to the front of the classroom. And they had to interact with each other in front of these two hundred students. I was there to insist that they practice the habits of effective interdependence—think win-win, seek first to understand, and synergize.

"Are you two willing to communicate until we can come up with a win-win solution?"

"I don't know what it would be! I don't feel they . . ."

"Wait a minute. You won't lose. You will both win."

"But how could that possibly be? One of us wins, the other loses."

"Are you willing to try to go for it? Remember not to capitulate. Don't give in. Don't compromise."

"I guess."

"Okay. Seek first to understand. You can't make your point until you restate his point to his satisfaction."

As they began to dialogue, they kept interrupting each other.

"Yeah. But don't you realize that . . ."

I said, "Wait a minute! I don't know if the other person feels understood. Do you feel understood?"

"Absolutely not."

"Okay. You can't make your point."

You cannot believe the sweat those people were in. They couldn't listen. They had each judged right off the bat because they took different positions.

Finally, after about forty-five minutes, they started to really listen. And you cannot imagine the effect upon them—personally, emotionally—and the effect upon the entire audience watching this process go on.

When they listened openly and empathetically to the underlying needs and the fears and the feeling of people on such a tender issue, it was a very powerful thing. The two people in front had tears in their eyes. Half the audience had tears in their eyes. They were categorically ashamed of how they had judged each other, labeled each other, and condemned all who thought differently. They were totally overwhelmed by the synergistic ideas that came out about what could be done. They came up with a number of alternatives, including new insights into prevention, adoption, and education. After two hours, each said of the other, "We had no idea that's what it meant to listen! Now we understand why they feel the way they do."[2]

There are a number of reasons we do not listen well. One has to do with our body's communication hardware. The brain is just too fast for the tongue. Most people speak at about 125 to 140 words per minute. Some announcers and professional speakers can speak comfortably in the 170 to 200 word range. The ear is able to listen to 400 words per minute, or more with a little training. The brain, our magnificent computer, is able to process information at a rate of 1,000 to 1,400 words per minute. Because of the difference in these rates, the brain is able to tune in for a fraction of a second and process the words the speaker said and then take a break and tune out before the next series of words arrives. That is exactly what poor listeners do—they allow their minds to tune out and wander.

Another problem is that most people have very short attention spans. According to a North Carolina study, most people only actively listen for about seventeen seconds at a time. The reason for this may be that we have grown accustomed to the electronic media's pandering to our laziness by trying to make every fact and option short and simple. The consumer today wants instant everything and is not very patient with preachers, politicians, news commentators, or speakers who expect them to think long and hard.

A third reason for our difficulty as listeners has to do with our education. The amount of training that we received in communication skills is inversely related to how much we use them. Most of us in our schooling have received the most training in writing, yet, on average, we write only nine percent of the time that we are communicating. The second greatest amount of training is in reading, and we use that only sixteen percent of the time. We receive even less training for speaking than for reading, yet we use speaking thirty percent of the time. Lastly, very few are trained to listen, and yet we use it forty-five percent of the time we are communicating.[3]

The busy employer comes to mind. While shuffling through a mound of paperwork, an employee comes in to ask a question.

"Can I speak to you for a moment?"

"What do you need?" the employer responds sharply.

Noticing that the employer continues to shuffle through papers, the employee answers, "I need your *heart* to listen."

How do we listen with our hearts? We do six things:

- First, we look and act, interested. We do not read our mail, doodle, shuffle, or tap paper while others are talking.
- Second, we observe nonverbal behavior, such as body language, to glean meaning beyond what is said to us.
- Third, we do not interrupt. We stay quiet past our tolerance level.
- Fourth, we listen between the lines, for implicit meanings as well as explicit ones. We consider connotations as well as denotations. We note figures of speech. Instead of accepting a person's remarks as the whole story, we listen for omissions—things left unsaid or unexplained, which should have been logically present. One of the most important aspects of listening is to hear what is *not* being said. We ask about these.
- Fifth, to ensure understanding, we rephrase what the other person has just told us at key points in the conversation.
- Sixth, we imagine the other person's viewpoint. We picture ourselves in her position, doing her work, facing her problems, using her language, and having her values. If the other person is younger or more junior, we remember what it was like when we were that age or in that position.

In her book called *The Listener*, Taylor Caldwell writes,

[We do] not need to go to the moon or other solar systems. [We do] not require bigger and better bombs and
missiles. [We] will not die if [we do] not get better hous-
ing or more vitamins . . . [Our] basic needs are few, and
it takes little to acquire them, in spite of advertisers.
[We] can survive on a small amount of bread in the
meanest shelter . . . But [our] real need, [our] most terri-
ble need is for someone to listen to [us], not as a patient,
but as a human soul.[4]

We honor one another when we listen to each other.

● *FIFTH, groups honor one another by respecting differing
  opinions.*
I first met Melanie in court. She was one of three young, aggres-
sive prosecuting attorneys. She was about seven months pregnant at
the time, yet she was tough as nails.
I had been invited to sit on the bench with an Orange County
judge as part of his efforts to expose leaders in the community to the
judicial system. The afternoon I sat next to the judge was an eye-
opener. We heard cases ranging from petty theft to assault to drug traf-
ficking. After hearing the scheduled cases for the day, the judge held a
debriefing session in his chambers. He gathered the public defenders
and the prosecuting attorneys who had been assigned to his court-
room, introduced me to them, and encouraged me to ask questions.
So, I did. I asked about case loads and office hours and how they bal-
anced career and family. I also asked them why they chose prosecuting
over defending or defending over prosecuting. I enjoyed my time "on
the bench."
Five months later, I met Melanie once again—this time in worship. She was looking for a church home for herself and her newborn
baby. She was also looking for a group that could handle her faith
questions, and she had a number of them. This tough, no-nonsense
prosecuting attorney asked me, "Is there a place here where I can say, 'I
don't believe that.' Is there a place in your church where I can say, 'I see
it differently'? Sometimes I sit in classes here and listen to people, and
they all nod and seem to be on the same page when I do not even have
the book. Is there a place where I can bring my questions and doubts
and not be ostracized from the group?"

We outdo one another in showing honor when we make room for others who do not see things as we may see them. In fact, some of my favorite groups have been those where people do not see things eye-to-eye. I love being in groups of Democrats and Republicans, pro-lifers and pro-choicers, religious conservatives and religious liberals because we have so much to teach each other and so much to learn from one another.

Unfortunately, some saints assume the role of the morality police, or the judge and jury of humankind, and squelch such healthy debate and diversity. In this regard John Killinger repeats a story he heard D. T. Niles tell at Princeton University:

> Sometime after World War II, during the reconstruction of Europe, the World Council of Churches wanted to see how its money was being spent in some remote parts of the Balkan peninsula. Accordingly it dispatched John Mackie, who was then the president of the Church of Scotland, and two brothers in the cloth of another denomination—a rather severe and pietistic denomination—to take a jeep and travel to some of the villages where the funds were being disbursed.
>
> One afternoon Dr. Mackie and the other two clergymen went to call on the Orthodox priest in a small Greek village. The priest was overjoyed to see them and was eager to pay his respects. Immediately, he produced a box of Havana cigars, a great treasure in those days, and offered each of his guests a cigar. Dr. Mackie took one, bit the end off, lit it, puffed a few puffs, and said how good it was. The other gentlemen looked horrified and said, "No, thank you, we don't smoke."
>
> Realizing he had somehow offended the two who refused, the priest was anxious to make amends. So he excused himself and reappeared in a few minutes with a flagon of his choicest wine. Dr. Mackie took a glassful, sniffed it like a connoisseur, sipped it, and praised its quality. Soon he asked for another glass. His companions, however, drew themselves back even more noticeably than before and said, "No, thank you, we don't drink!"
>
> Later, when the three men were in the jeep again, making their way up the rough road out of the village,

the two pious clergymen turned upon Dr. Mackie with a vengeance. "Dr. Mackie," they insisted, "do you mean to tell us that you are the president of the Church of Scotland and an officer of the World Council of Churches and you smoke and drink?"

Dr. Mackie had had all he could take, and his Scottish temper got the better of him. "No, dammit, I don't," he said, "but somebody had to be a Christian."[5]

It is easy to define "authentic Christian spirituality" according to our particular experience or expression of it. It is more difficult to define it in terms of respecting different viewpoints. Yet, that is what healthy groups do. Healthy groups honor people with divergent opinions.

GROUP DISCUSSION AND SHARING

1. **Icebreaker** (20-30 minutes)
    - What was a high point and a low point from your past week?
    - Since this is the last study in this book, think back over the previous chapters. What "one another" practice particularly stood out for you?

2. **Discussion** (15-25 minutes)
    - Give your group a letter grade (A,B,C, D or F) in the following five categories:
        ___ Beginning and ending on time.
        ___ Meeting with the people present.
        ___ Doing the assigned homework.
        ___ Listening attentively.
        ___ Respecting differing opinions.
    - Based on your assessment of your group, what is one thing you would like to see your group do differently? What is one thing you hope your group never stops doing?

GROUP COVENANT

1. The reason our group exists is _____

   _____

2. We will meet ____ times (s) a month, and this covenant will be in effect for ____ weeks/months. At the end of the covenant period, we will evaluate our progress and growth.

3. We will meet on _____ (day of the week), from _____ A.M/P.M To _____ A.M/P.M.

4. Our meeting will take place at

   _____ .

5. We will study _____ .

6. _____ will lead the sessions.

7. A typical schedule for the group will be:

   _____

   _____

   _____

   _____

8. We will agree to the following disciplines:
   Attendance: We will be here whenever possible.
   Ownership: We will share responsibility for the group.
   Accountability: We give permission to the other group members to hold us accountable for goals we set for ourselves.
   Confidentiality: We agree to keep in the group what is shared in the group.

9. Our plan for service includes:

10. Our plan for fun and recreation includes:

Signed: _____

- The end of a study is a good time to evaluate your continued participation. Do you want to continue or is it time to leave the group? For those who decide to leave, thank God for your time together and allow them to go with your blessing. For those who want to continue, plan on having a "covenanting" session *the next time* you meet. A sample group covenant is shown on the facing page

  Once again, work on your covenant *the next time* you meet. At *this* meeting say good-bye to those who have decided to leave the group.

3. **Sharing Prayer Concerns** *(20-30 minutes)*

4. **Pray** *(5-10 minutes)*
    Pray for all in the group, but especially those who will be leaving. Thank God for them and the gifts they have brought to the group.

Notes

Introduction
1. Bob Greene, *All Summer Long*, 30-31.

Chapter 1: The Power of Community
1. Bill Moyers, *Healing and the Mind*, 105.
2. Ibid., 356.
3. Robert Fulghum, *All I Really Need to Know I Learned in Kindergarten*, 58.
4. Reginald Heber, "Holy, Holy, Holy, Lord God Almighty!" *The Presbyterian Hymnal*, 138.
5. Gareth Weldon Icenogle, *Biblical Foundations for Small Group Ministry*, 21.
6. Bruce Larson, *My Creator, My Friend*, 26.
7. P.S. Minear, "Church, idea of," *The Interpreter's Dictionary of the Bible, Vol. 1.*
8. As quoted in "Standing in the Crossfire: Interview with Bill Hybels," *Leadership: A Practical Journal for Church Leaders*, Winter 1993, 14.
9. Robert Wuthrow, *Sharing the Journey*, 54.

Chapter 2: Meet Together
1. E. F. Scott, as quoted by William Barclay, *The Daily Bible Study Series: The Letter to the Hebrews*, xvii.
2. Stephen R. Covey, A. Roger Merrill and Rebecca R. Merrill, *First Things First*, 88.
3. Lyman Coleman, ed. *Serendipity Bible for Groups.*

Chapter 3: Accept One Another
1. Dale E. Galloway, *20/20 Vision*, 74.
2. Bruce Larson, *30 Days to a New You*, 102.
3. Arthur M. Friedrichs, "Judgement," *The Upper Room*, August 24, 1994.
4. C.S. Lewis, *The Voyage of the Dawn Treader*, 132-136.

Chapter 4: Serve One Another
1. As quoted in "Service/Sacrifice,"*The Preacher's Illustration Service, Vol. 9*, November 1996, 9.
2. As quoted by David McKechnie, *Experiencing God's Pleasure*, 46.
3. Bryant S. Hinckley, *Not By Bread Alone*, 25.
4. As quoted by Charles R. Swindoll, *Improving Your Serve*, 19.
5. As quoted by Calvin Miller, "From Entertainment to Servanthood," *Preaching Today*, Tape No. 132.
6. Sermon of David McKellips, "Clearing Away the Clutter," *Church Leaders Manual*, A-76.
7. Richard A. Swenson, *Margin*, 74.
8. David L. McKenna, *The Communicator's Commentary, Vol. 2: Mark*, 54.

Chapter 5: Be Kind to One Another

1. As quoted in "Christmas/Hope/Judgment," *The Preacher's Illustration Service, Vol. 7,* November/December 1994, 4.

Chapter 6: Teach One Another

1. As cited by Herb Miller, *The Vital Congregation,* 93-94.
2. Herb Miller, *The Vital Congregation,* 93-94.
3. William Ophuls, *Ecology and the Politics of Scarcity,* 185.
4. Lewis Carroll, *Alice in Wonderland,* 88-89.
5. C. S. Lewis, *Mere Christianity,* 174-175.
6. Alan Jones, *Exploring Spiritual Direction,* 57.
7. As cited by David Roper, *Psalm 23,* 124.
8. "To verify . . .," *Leadership: A Practical Journal for Church Leaders,* Summer 1993, Vol. XIV, 76.
9. Barry Woodbridge, *A Guidebook for Spiritual Friends,* 29.
10. As quoted by Jack Canfield and Mark Victor Hansen, *Chicken Soup for the Soul,* 144-147.

Chapter 7: Live in Harmony with One Another

1. Brian Buhler, "The Ultimate Community," *Preaching Today,* Tape No. 146.
2. "To illustrate . . .," *Leadership: A Practical Journal for Church Leaders,* Fall 1992, Vol. XIII, 47.
3. R. E. Nixon, "Glory," *The New Bible Dictionary,* 472.
4. William Barclay, *The Daily Bible Study Series, Vol. 2: The Gospel of John,* 255.
5. As quoted by Wayne Brouwer, "Harmony," *Leadership: A Practical Journal for Church Leaders,* Vol. XVII, Spring 1996, 68.
6. Joseph Aldrich, *Life-Style Evangelism,* 133.
7. Ibid., 135.
8. Bill Hybels and Mark Mittleberg, *Becoming A Contagious Christian,* 167.
9. As quoted by Maxie Dunnam, *Alive in Christ,* 94.
10. Martin Bolt and David Myers, *The Human Connection,* 95.
11. As quoted by Charles R. Swindoll, *Laugh Again,* 186.
12. As quoted in "Turning Vision into Reality: An Interview with Ken Blanchard," *Leadership: A Practical Journal for Church Leaders,* Vol. XVII, Spring 1996, 116.

Chapter 8: Forgive One Another

1. Daniel Ledwith, "Forgiveness: An Attempt to Discover Forgiveness in the Web of Reformed Theology," presented to Dr. Frank A. James III, Reformed Theological Seminary, Maitland, Florida, May 27, 1997 in fulfillment of independent study course.
2. Ps. 78:38, Jer. 18:23, Duet. 21:8
3. Norman Vincent Peale, "How to Find Health of Mind & Body," *A Treasury of Courage and Confidence.*
4. Karl Menninger, *Whatever Became of Sin?,* 13.
5. Bill Watterson, *Something Under the Bed Is Drooling,* 69.

Chapter 9: Do Not Envy One Another

1. *Webster's Ninth New Collegiate Dictionary*, 417.
2. As quoted by Os Guinness in the Foreword to "The Revenge of Failure," *The Trinity Forum Reading*, Spring 1994, 6.
3. As quoted by Hesketh Pearson, ed., *Oscar Wilde: His Life and Wit*.
4. Henrie Fairlie, "The Revenge of Failure," *The Trinity Forum Reading*, Spring 1994, 10.
5. *The Orlando Sentinel* (Orlando), September 7, 1997, A-16.
6. Anthony Campolo, *Seven Deadly Sins*, 106.
7. *Omaha World-Herald* (Omaha), April 29, 1991, A-1,2.

Chapter 10: Be Hospitable to One Another

1. William White, as quoted in "A Party for Coats," *Parables, Etc.*, October 1990, 2.
2. *Webster's Ninth New Collegiate Dictionary*, 583.
3. C. Peter Wagner, *Your Spiritual Gifts Can Help Your Church Grow*, 70.
4. Karen Mains, *Open Heart, Open Home*.
5. Bruce Bugbee, *Networking*, 45b.
6. V. H. Kooy, "Hospitality," *The Interpreter's Dictionary of the Bible, Vol. 2*, 654.
7. Herb Miller, *How to Build a Magnetic Church*, 63.
8. As quoted by Herb Miller, *How to Build a Magnetic Church*, 64.

Chapter 11: Honor One Another

1. As quoted in "Respect in Marriage," *Parables, Etc.*, October 1995, 2.
2. Stephen Covey, A. Roger Merrill, and Rebecca Merrill, *First Things First*, 232-233.
3. Hal Jenks, "Why Don't We Listen," *Net Results*, November 1995, 16-17.
4. As quoted in "Listening/Compassion," *The Preachers Illustration Service*, November/December 1995, 7.
5. John Killinger, "When We Stop Being Free," *Pulpit Digest*, July/August 1992, 12-13.

Bibliography

BOOKS & COMMENTARIES

Aldrich, Joseph. *Life-Style Evangelism*. Portland, OR: Multnomah Press, 1981.

Barclay, William. *The Daily Study Bible Series, Vol. 2: The Gospel of John*. Philadelphia: Westminster, 1956.

_____. *The Daily Study Bible Series: The Letter to the Hebrews*. Philadelphia: Westminster, 1957.

Bolt, Martin and David Myers. *The Human Connection*. Downers Grove, IL: InterVarsity Press, 1984.

Bugbee, Bruce. *Networking: Equipping Those Who Are Seeking to Serve*. Pasadena, CA: Charles E. Fuller Institute, 1989.

Campolo, Anthony. *Seven Deadly Sins*. Wheaton, IL: Victor Books, 1989.

Canfield, Jack and Mark Victor Hansen. *Chicken Soup for the Soul*. Deerfield Beach, FL: Health Communications, 1993.

Carroll, Lewis. *Alice in Wonderland*, ed. Donald J. Gray. New York: W.W. Norton & Co. Inc., 1971.

Coleman, Lyman, ed. *Serendipity Bible for Groups*. Littleton, CO: Serendipity House, 1988.

Covey, Stephen R., A. Roger Merrill and Rebecca R. Merrill. *First Things First*. New York: Simon and Schuster, 1994.

Dunnam, Maxie. *Alive in Christ: The Dynamic Process of Spiritual Formation*. Nashville: Abingdon, 1982.

Fulghum, Robert. *All I Really Need to Know I Learned in Kindergarten*. New York: Villard Books, 1989.

Galloway, Dale E. *20/20 Vision: How to Create a Successful Church with Lay Pastors and Cell Groups*. Portland, OR: Scott Publishing, 1986.

Greene, Bob. *All Summer Long*. New York: Doubleday, 1993.

Hinckley, Bryant S. *Not By Bread Alone*. Salt Lake City, UT: Bookcraft, 1955.

Hybels, Bill and Mark Mittleberg. *Becoming a Contagious Christian*. Grand Rapids, MI: Zondervan, 1994.

Icenogle, Gareth Weldon. *Biblical Foundations for Small Group Ministry: An Intergenerational Approach*. Downers Grove, IL: InterVarsity Press, 1994.

The Interpreter's Dictionary of the Bible, Vols. 1 and 2. Nashville: Abingdon, 1962.

Jones, Alan. *Exploring Spiritual Direction*. Minneapolis, MN: Seabury Press, 1982.

Larson, Bruce. *My Creator, My Friend: The Genesis of a Relationship*. Waco, TX: Word Books, 1986.

_____. *30 Days to a New You*. Garden Grove, CA: Crystal Cathedral Ministries, 1994.

Lewis, C. S. *Mere Christianity*. New York: The MacMillan Company, 1972.

_____. *The Voyage of the Dawn Treader*. New York: Collier Books, 1970.

Mains, Karen. *Open Heart, Open Home*. Elgin, IL: David C. Cook, 1976.

McKechnie, David. *Experiencing God's Pleasure*. Nashville: Nelson, 1989.

McKenna, David L. *The Communicator's Commentary Series, Vol. 2: Mark*. Waco, TX: Word Books, 1982.

Menninger, Karl. *Whatever Became of Sin?* New York: Hawthorne, 1973.

Meyer, Richard C. *One Anothering, Volume I: Biblical Building Blocks for Small Groups*. Philadelphia: Innisfree Press, 1990.

Miller, Herb. *How to Build a Magnetic Church*. Nashville, Abingdon, 1987.

_____ . *The Vital Congregation*. Nashville: Abingdon, 1990.

Moyers, Bill. *Healing and the Mind*. New York: Doubleday, 1993.

The New Bible Dictionary, J.D. Douglas, ed. Grand Rapids, MI: Eerdmans, 1973.

Ophuls, William. *Ecology and the Politics of Scarcity*. San Francisco: W.H. Freeman & Co., 1977.

Peale, Norman Vincent, ed. *A Treasury of Courage and Confidence*. New York: K.S. Giniger Co., Inc., 1970.

Pearson, Hesketh. *Oscar Wilde: His Life and Wit*. New York: Harper & Brothers, 1946.

Roper, David. *Psalm 23: The Song of a Passionate Heart*. Grand Rapids, MI: Discovery House, 1994.

Swenson, Richard A. *Margin*. Colorado Springs: NavPress, 1992.

Swindoll, Charles R. *Improving Your Serve*. Waco, TX: Word Books, 1981.

_____ . *Laugh Again*. Dallas, TX: Word Books, 1992.

Wagner, C. Peter. *Your Spiritual Gifts Can Help Your Church Grow*. Glendale, CA: Regal Books, 1974.

Watterson, Bill. *Something Under the Bed Is Drooling*. Kansas City: Andrews and McMeel, 1988.

Woodbridge, Barry. *A Guidebook for Spiritual Friends*. Nashville: The Upper Room, 1985.

Wuthrow, Robert. *Sharing the Journey: Support Groups and America's New Quest for Community*. New York: Free Press, 1994.

ARTICLES

Brouwer, Wayne. "Harmony," *Leadership: A Practical Journal for Church Leaders*, Spring 1996. Carol Stream, IL: Christianity Today.

"Christmas/Hope/Judgment," *The Preacher's Illustration Service, Vol. 7*, November/December 1994. Ventnor, NJ: Italicus, Inc.

Fairlie, Henrie. "The Revenge of Failure," *The Trinity Forum Reading*, Spring 1994. Burke, VA: The Trinity Forum.

Friedrichs, Arthur M. "Judgement," *The Upper Room*. August 24, 1994. Nashville: The Upper Room.

Guinness, Os. Foreword to "The Revenge of Failure," *The Trinity Forum Reading*, Spring 1994. Burke, VA: The Trinity Forum.

Jenks, Hal. "Why Don't We Listen?" *Net Results*, November 1995. Lubbock, TX: Net Results.

Killinger, John. "When We Stop Being Free," *Pulpit Digest*, July/August, 1992.

"Listening/Compassion," *The Preacher's Illustration Service, Vol. 8*, November/December 1995. Ventnor, NJ: Italicus, Inc.

McKellips, David. "Clearing Away the Clutter," *Church Leaders Manual*. Wheaton, IL: Chapel of the Air Ministries, 1995.

"A Party for Coats," *Parables, Etc.*, October 1990. Platteville, CO: Saratoga Press.

"Respect in Marriage," *Parables, Etc.*. October 1995. Platteville, CO: Saratoga Press.

"Service/Sacrifice," *The Preacher's Illustration Service, Vol. 9*, November 1996. Ventnor, NJ: Italicus, Inc.

"Standing in the Crossfire: Interview with Bill Hybels," *Leadership: A Practical Journal for Church Leader,*. Winter 1993. Carol Stream, IL: Christianity Today.

"To illustrate . . ." *Leadership: A Practical Journal for Church Leaders*, Fall 1992. Carol Stream, IL: Christianity Today.

"To verify . . . " *Leadership: A Practical Journal for Church Leaders*, Spring 1993. Carol Stream, IL: Christianity Today.

"Turning Vision into Reality: An Interview with Ken Blanchard," *Leadership: A Practical Journal for Church Leaders*, Spring 1996. Carol Stream, IL: Christianity Today.

TAPES

Buhler, Brian. "The Ultimate Community," *Preaching Today*, Tape No. 146. Carol Stream, IL: Christianity Today.

Miller, Calvin. "From Entertainment to Servanthood," *Preaching Today*, Tape No. 132. Carol Stream, IL: Christianity Today.

PERMISSION ACKNOWLEDGMENTS

Abingdon Press, for the quotation from *How to Build a Magnetic Church* by Herb Miller. Copyright © 1987 Abingdon Press. Used by permission.

Wayne Brouwer, for the quotation from "Taming the Beast" from *Preaching Today*.

Brian Buhler, for the quotation from "The Ultimate Community" from *Preaching Today*.

Anthony Campolo, for the quotation from *Seven Deadly Sins*. Published by ChariotVictor Publishing. Copyright © 1987 by Anthony Campolo.

Christianity Today, for the quotation from "Turning Vision into Reality: An Interview with Ken Blanchard." *Leadership: A Practical Journal for Church Leaders*, Spring 1996.

Christianity Today, for the quotation by Emo Philips. *Leadership: A Practical Journal for Church Leaders*, Spring 1996.

Wm. B. Eerdmans Publishing Co., for the quotation from "Glory," from *The New Bible Dictionary*, J.D. Douglas, ed., copyright © The Inter-Varsity Fellowship, 1962, Wm. B. Eerdmans Publishing Company.

Arthur M Friedrichs, for the quotation from "Judgement" from *The Upper Room – Daily Devotional Guide*, August 1994.

Dale E. Galloway, for the quotation from *20/20 Vision: How to Create a Successful Church with Lay Pastors and Cell Groups*. Published by Scott Publishing. Copyright © 1986.

K. S. Giniger Co., Inc., for the quotation from *A Treasury of Courage and Confidence*, Ed. By Norman Vincent Peale, © 1970 Norman Vincent Peale.

HarperCollins Publishers Ltd., for the quotation from *Mere Christianity* by C. S. Lewis. Copyright © 1972.

Health Communications, Inc., for the quotations from *Chicken Soup for the Soul* by Jack Canfield and Mark Victor Hansen. Copyright © 1993 by Health Communications, Inc.

William M. Kinnard, for the quotation from *Joy Comes with the Morning*, Word Books. Copyright © 1979.

Bruce Larson, for the quotation from *My Creator, My Friend: The Genesis of a Relationship*. Published by Word Books. Copyright © 1986.

National Council of the Churches of Christ in the U.S.A., for the Scripture quotations from the *New Revised Standard Version Bible*. Copyright © 1989 by the Division of Christian Education of the National Council of the Churches of Christ in the U.S.A. Used by permission. All rights reserved.

NavPress/Pinon Press, for the quotation from *Margin* by Richard A. Swenson. Copyright © 1992. Used by permission of NavPress/Pinon Press.

Simon & Schuster, Inc., for the quotations from *First Things First* by Stephen R. Covey. Copyright © 1994 by Stephen R. Covey, A. Roger Merrill and Rebecca R. Merrill. Reprinted by permission of Simon & Schuster, Inc.

Upper Room Books, for the quotation from *A Guidebook for Spiritual Friends* by Barry A. Woodbridge. Copyright © 1985 by the Upper Room. Used by permission of Upper Room Books.

Zondervan Publishing House, for the quotation from *Becoming a Contagious Christian* by Bill Hybels and Mark Mittleberg. Copyright © 1994 by Bill Hybels and Mark Mittleberg. Used by permission of Zondervan Publishing House.

Zondervan Publishing House, for the quotations from the *Holy Bible, New International Version*. Copyright © 1973, 1987, 1984 International Bible Society. Used by permission of Zondervan Bible Publishers.

RICHARD C. MEYER

RICHARD C. MEYER served the church in pastoral ministry for 25 years. He has pastored small (250 members), medium (800 members), and large (1275 members) congregations in the Presbyterian church. In the fall of 2000, he left pastoral ministry to follow his passion of calling people into deep spiritual community through small groups. He currently is devoting his energies to the formation of The One Anothering Institute, a consulting resource for churches.

Meyer is a much sought-after conference speaker and small group consultant, chairperson of the Faith at Work Board, and a regular columnist for the *Faith @ Work Magazine*. His *One Anothering* series has been called "the best book on church groups I have ever seen!"